WEEKEND
WOODWORKING
FOR THE GARDEN

WEEKEND
WOODWORKING
FOR THE GARDEN

STERLING PUBLISHING CO., INC.
NEW YORK

■ART AND PRODUCTION
Thomas Gaines

■PHOTOGRAPHY
Evan Bracken

■PHOTO STYLIST
Skip Wade

■ILLUSTRATIONS
Orrin Lundgren

■ASSISTANT EDITOR
Amy Cook

■EDITORIAL INTERN
Jan Menon

FOR MOM AND DAD

Library of Congress Cataloging-in-Publication Data Available

10   9   8   7   6   5   4   3

First paperback edition published in 2001 by
Sterling Publishing Company, Inc.
387 Park Avenue South
New York, N.Y. 10016

Created and produced by Altamont Press, Inc.
50 College Street, Asheville, NC 28801

© 2000 by Sterling Publishing Company, Inc.

Distributed in Canada by Sterling Publishing c/o Canadian Manda Group,
    One Atlantic Avenue, Suite 105, Toronto, Ontario, Canada M6K 3E7
Distributed in Great Britain and Europe by Chrysalis Books
64 Brewery Road, London N7 9NT, England
Distributed in Australia by Capricorn Link (Australia) Pty Ltd.
    P.O. Box 704, Windsor, NSW 2756 Australia

Printed in China

Sterling ISBN 0-8069-2048-3 Trade
           0-8069-2253-2 Paper

TABLE OF CONTENTS

INTRODUCTION

If you've always longed to fill your backyard and garden with handsome furnishings and useful gadgets, but didn't think you had the money to buy them or the expertise and time to build them, you've picked up the right book. *Weekend Woodworking for the Garden* is packed with more than 20 great projects that anyone who can hold a saw and drive a screw can build. Even if you've never worked with wood before, you can make a good-looking garden bench (page 119), a handy tool holder (page 78), a cozy butterfly box (page 36), or any of the other projects in this book—in just a day or two.

You won't need expensive tools or hard-to-find materials, either. You can build every project in this book with simple tools and standard lumber. Your local lumberyard will carry most of the wood you need, and you probably already own many of the basic tools.

Still not convinced that a beginning woodworker can create something as stunning as the arbor-bench combination on the facing page? Turn to page 56 and browse through its complete lists of required materials, supplies, and hardware. Take a look at its comprehensive, exploded-view illustrations. Read over its easy-to-follow, step-by-step instructions. We think you'll agree that even a first-time woodworker can put together this gorgeous project.

That's because we developed this book with one goal in mind: to make the craft of woodworking for the outdoors accessible to everyone. If you're a complete novice to woodworking, read over the first chapter, "Woodworking Basics." In it, you'll find a brief introduction to all of the basic information required to build the projects in this book. If you're a more experienced woodworker, be sure to read through the project instructions carefully before beginning; you'll probably want to "translate" our instructions for your more advanced tools and knowledge.

Whatever your level of skill, you're sure to find projects that are just right for your garden and backyard. Let your neighbor buy a mass-manufactured trellis; your climbing vines will inhabit a one-of-a-kind creation that you built with your own hands. And because you'll only need a day or two to build it, you'll still have plenty of time left for gardening!

WOODWORKING BASICS

If you've never worked with wood before, or if your woodworking skills are a little rusty, take a few minutes to read through this chapter. In it you'll find brief introductions to all of the materials, tools, and techniques you'll need to build the projects in the pages that follow. If you're still unsure about something, enlist the help of a friend who has plenty of woodworking experience, or check out a basic woodworking-techniques book from your local library. Never hesitate to consult experts! Most craftspeople enjoy sharing their skills with people who are eager to learn them. Of course, every expert has a certain way of doing things, so don't be alarmed if three different woodworkers show you three different ways to perform the same task. Just remember to always keep safety uppermost in your mind as you develop your personal woodworking style. (See page 11 for basic safety tips.)

LUMBER

SOFTWOODS AND HARDWOODS

Most lumber is divided into softwoods and hardwoods. Softwoods come from fast-growing, coniferous evergreen trees such as pine, spruce, and redwood. Hardwoods come from slower-growing, typically broad-leaved, deciduous trees such as oak, maple, and ash.

Both classes of wood have their advantages. Softwoods tend to be softer, lighter, and easier to cut than hardwoods; many are also less expensive and more readily available. Hardwoods usually offer greater rot resistance and durability, and many people find them more attractive than softwoods.

LUMBER DIMENSIONS

You'll buy softwoods as dimension lumber, boards that have been dried, planed (or surfaced) to a standard thickness, and cut to a standard width. These processes can reduce a board's original dimensions by as much as three-quarters of an inch.

A deciduous forest

A coniferous forest

The confusing thing about dimension lumber is that it's named for its nominal (pre-dried, pre-planed) thickness and width. If you ask for a 2 x 4 (pronounced "two by four"), you won't actually get a board that's 2 inches thick and 4 inches wide; instead, you'll get a board that's $1\frac{1}{2}$ inches thick and $3\frac{1}{2}$ inches wide. However, if you ask for a 2 x 4 that's 8 feet long, you will get an 8-foot-long board. The chart to the right gives nominal and actual sizes for softwood lumber.

A type of dimension lumber that you won't find listed in the chart, but that you will need for several projects in this book is $\frac{5}{4}$ x 6 ("five-quarter by six") bull-nosed decking, or just decking. This is pressure-treated (see page 14) wood that's been planed to a thickness of between 1 inch and $1\frac{1}{4}$ inches, and a width of between $5\frac{1}{2}$ inches and 6 inches. It's called "bull-nosed" because its edges have been rounded. Decking is generally used for (as you may have guessed) building decks.

Fortunately, you won't need a chart to buy hardwoods —but you may need a calculator. Hardwoods are sold in standard thicknesses, but random widths and lengths; sawmills cut them this way to maximize the amount of usable lumber from each log. Thus, hardwoods are sold by the board foot, a unit of measure equivalent to a piece of wood 1 inch thick and 1 foot square. To calculate the board feet in a given piece of lumber, multiply its thickness (in inches) by its width (in inches); then multiply that number by the board's length (in feet). Divide the result by 12.

The one thing you might find a little tricky at first is that hardwood thicknesses are measured in $\frac{1}{4}$-inch increments and expressed as fractions; for instance, a $1\frac{1}{4}$-inch-thick board is called $\frac{5}{4}$ (pronounced "five quarter") stock. The standard hardwood thicknesses are: $\frac{3}{4}$, $\frac{4}{4}$, $\frac{5}{4}$, $\frac{6}{4}$, and $\frac{8}{4}$. Don't worry if you're not good with fractions; the people at your local lumberyard will be happy to help you with any calculations.

Softwood Lumber Sizes

The softwood boards you buy at a lumberyard or home-improvement center—the ones you hear described as 2 x 4s or 1 x 6s—don't actually measure 2 inches by 4 inches or 1 inch by 6 inches. Their actual (as opposed to "nominal") dimensions are approximately $1\frac{1}{2}$ inches by $3\frac{1}{2}$ inches and $\frac{3}{4}$ inch by $5\frac{1}{2}$ inches. Before you begin building, familiarize yourself with the differences between nominal and actual measurements.

Nominal	Actual
1 x 2	$\frac{3}{4}$" x $1\frac{1}{2}$"
1 x 4	$\frac{3}{4}$" x $3\frac{1}{2}$"
1 x 6	$\frac{3}{4}$" x $5\frac{1}{2}$"
1 x 8	$\frac{3}{4}$" x $7\frac{1}{4}$"
1 x 10	$\frac{3}{4}$" x $9\frac{1}{4}$"
1 x 12	$\frac{3}{4}$" x $11\frac{1}{4}$"
2 x 2	$1\frac{1}{2}$" x $1\frac{1}{2}$"
2 x 4	$1\frac{1}{2}$" x $3\frac{1}{2}$"
2 x 6	$1\frac{1}{2}$" x $5\frac{1}{2}$"
2 x 8	$1\frac{1}{2}$" x $7\frac{1}{4}$"
2 x 10	$1\frac{1}{2}$" x $9\frac{1}{4}$"
2 x 12	$1\frac{1}{2}$" x $11\frac{1}{4}$"
4 x 4	$3\frac{1}{2}$" x $3\frac{1}{2}$"
4 x 6	$3\frac{1}{2}$" x $5\frac{1}{2}$"
6 x 6	$5\frac{1}{2}$" x $5\frac{1}{2}$"
8 x 8	$7\frac{1}{2}$" x $7\frac{1}{2}$"

Also note that boards of the same nominal size can vary as much as $\frac{1}{8}$" in width or thickness. Plywood measurements, because the sheets are sanded at the mill, can also be thinner than its nominal size. Measuring lumber before you buy it will save troublesome errors during assembly.

-SAFETY-

Woodworking can be a relaxing, rewarding hobby. It can also be a dangerous one if you don't take a few simple precautions.

▶ Work with wood and tools only when you're completely alert and able to concentrate on what you're doing. Running a power saw when you're worn out or mentally raging at your boss is not a safe habit!

▶ Dress for the occasion. Fast-moving blades can catch on loose sleeves, skirts, ties, and untucked shirts, so wear close-fitting, comfortable clothes. Leave jewelry outside the shop, and if you have long hair, tie it into a ponytail.

▶ Sharp tools are safer tools. They require less force to do their work, so controlling their actions is easier. Learn how sharp the edges of your tools should be; then keep them in that condition.

▶ Before turning on a piece of power equipment, clear any obstacles—including power cords, sawhorses, and other tools—from both the top and bottom of the work piece.

▶ Never stand in the path of a power saw—do not stand directly behind it or directly in front of it. Power saws can throw pieces of wood with incredible force, and you don't want to be in the way if that happens.

▶ Keep a pair of safety glasses nearby, and wear them whenever you make a cut or drill a hole.

▶ Protect your lungs, too. An inexpensive dust mask will filter out most of the harmful particles that result from cutting and sanding wood. Cut pressure-treated lumber (page 14) and apply finishes outside. If you must work with pressure-treated lumber or do finishing work indoors, wear a respirator.

▶ Wear earplugs when operating power tools; the whine of a circular saw or power drill can damage your hearing.

▶ Kids can learn a lot in a workshop, but if you can't give them your undivided attention, ask them to play outside while you work.

LUMBER GRADES

Within the categories of softwoods and hardwoods, the quality of lumber varies greatly. So how can you know if you're getting lumber that's the right quality for your project? You check its grade.

Lumber producers give wood a grade according to the number of defects in a given board. The illustrations to the right show some common flaws they look for; you'll want to check for these too, as you select your wood.

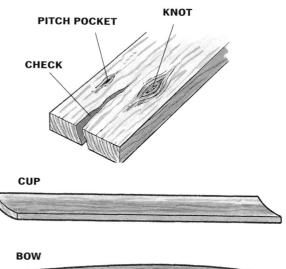

> ► **KNOTS** occur when lumber is cut through a branch or limb. Small, tight ones shouldn't be a problem for most outdoor projects, but avoid lumber with large, loose knots; they can fall out, leaving a big hole in your bench or planter.
>
> ► **CHECKS** along a board's length can split your lumber in half. If you see a split end, saw it off; just be sure that you have enough material to make up for the waste.
>
> ► **PITCH POCKETS** happen when sticky resinous material accumulates in one spot; this defect is most common in softwoods.
>
> ► **WARP** is called a **BOW** when it occurs across a board's length and a **CUP** when it occurs along the width. The type of warp called **TWIST** is, as you can see from the illustration, just what you'd expect. Check for warp by looking along a board down its length from one end and across its width from one edge.

Although both softwoods and hardwoods are susceptible to all these defects, the two types of lumber are categorized according to different grading systems. The tables that follow outline some typical lumber grades.

Hardwood Lumber Grades

FIRSTS are almost completely clear on both faces; they are suitable for very fine furniture and natural finishes.

SECONDS are quite clear on both faces and also suitable for most fine furniture and natural finishes.

"FIRST AND SECONDS" is a term that refers to a collection of lumber that contains at least 20% firsts. This is the highest grade of hardwood lumber that you're likely to find widely available, and it's abbreviated "FAS."

SELECTS are very clear on one face; the other face is not graded. They can be used for fine furniture, but you'll incur some waste.

NO. 1 COMMON lumber is about two-thirds clear on one face. It's suitable for less demanding furniture and for pieces that will be painted.

NO. 2 COMMON lumber is one-half clear on one face. You'll probably want to paint projects made from this grade.

Softwood Lumber Grades

SELECT GRADES

A-GRADE lumber is nearly flawless. It's suitable for natural finishes and is used in cabinetry (the making of fine wooden furniture).

B-GRADE lumber may contain a few small defects, but it's also suitable for natural finishes and cabinetry.

C-GRADE lumber contains defects that can be easily covered by paint.

D-GRADE lumber will have a few more flaws than C-grade, but all can be concealed with paint.

COMMON GRADES

NO. 1 COMMON lumber is free from warping, splits, and knotholes, although it may have a few tight knots.

NO. 2 COMMON lumber may have loose knots and a few blemishes, but won't have knotholes.

NO. 3 COMMON lumber may have defects of all types, including larger knots and small knotholes. Many of the defects can be removed, but you'll incur some waste.

NO. 4 COMMON lumber contains large knotholes and is used only for construction.

NO. 5 COMMON lumber is used only when appearance and strength aren't important.

STRUCTURAL GRADE lumbers are more than 2 inches thick and are used primarily for construction.

The higher the grade of lumber, the higher the price tag it will bear. Don't spend more money than you have to! Basically, lumber grades describe the size of useable pieces that you're likely to obtain from a board. If you're making a project with only small parts, such as the hanging wine chiller (page 96), you can use a lower grade of lumber than if you're making a large project such as the picnic table and bench combination (page 108). Remember, wood is all firsts between the flaws!

WEATHER RESISTANCE

Your project, budget, and personal taste will all help determine the type of wood you choose. For the projects in this book, a wood's ability to resist the rigors of garden life should be one of your primary concerns. All the things that make your garden an inviting home for plants can make it an equally uninviting place for wood. If you don't take preventive steps, sun, rain, insects—even that gourmet mulch mix that does wonders for your geraniums—will all assault your wooden garden projects.

The best way to protect your projects is to avoid placing them on grass or dirt for an extended period of time. Of course, garden projects are supposed to live outdoors, and many may have to be in direct contact with the ground. Although all wood will eventually succumb to rot and decay, you do have several options for increasing the weather resistance of your handiwork. These include using naturally weather-resistant lumber, chemically treated lumber (see the following page), and the application of protective finishes (see pages 31–32). The project shown in the photo below demonstrates how the elements can eat away at poorly protected wood.

The effects of outdoor elements on insufficiently protected wood

Naturally Weather-Resistant Lumber

Projects made from naturally decay- and rot-resistant hardwoods would make beautiful, durable additions to any garden; they'd also be a speedy way to rid your wallet of extra cash. If you'd like to build with naturally weather-resistant wood, specialty softwoods such as redwood, cypress, and cedar all combine the beauty and durability of hardwoods with the (relative) economy and availability of softwoods.

Treated Lumber

Many softwoods can be made more weather resistant by means of a waterborne application of chemical salts that is forced, under pressure, into the wood's cells. Wood that has undergone this process is called pressure-treated (PT) lumber, and it will last five to ten times longer than untreated wood. Almost all commercial lumberyards carry PT wood, which is sold in the same sizes as standard dimension lumber (page 10).

Manufacturers classify pressure-treated wood by whether it will be used aboveground or will be in direct contact with the ground. Lumber that's appropriate for ground contact has received a more intense level of treatment, which makes it more durable. Although it's more expensive, PT lumber treated for ground contact is the best pressure-treated option for the projects in this book.

If you choose to work with PT lumber, remember that it contains potentially harmful chemicals. Protect yourself by wearing leather gloves and a dust mask or a respirator when you cut treated wood. Wash your hands after handling it, launder your work clothes separately, and never burn the scraps.

PLYWOOD

Plywood is made from very thin layers of wood (called plies or veneers) glued together with the grain of each successive layer arranged at right angles to the last. It's sold in 4-foot-by-8-foot sheets, although some stores sell 4-foot-by-4-foot half-sheets.

Plywood can be made from softwoods, hardwoods, or a combination of both, and is classified as either veneer-core or lumber-core. The first type consists entirely of plies; the second has a core of lumber strips, sandwiched between sheets of veneer. Although veneer-core is stronger, lumber-core is the easier of the two to work with because its edges can be cut in the same manner as solid wood; the edges of veneer-core plywood tend to splinter and must be covered or filled.

Both types of plywood are graded "A" through "D," with the grade referring to the quality of the outer, face veneers; a grade of "A" represents the highest quality. Each sheet receives a grade for both faces, so an "A-B" piece has one face that's "A" quality and one that's "B" quality.

Plywood is also graded as either "interior" or "exterior." The main difference between the two is that the plies in exterior-grade plywood are held together with a waterproof adhesive. Use exterior-grade plywood for the projects in this book.

A couple of the projects in this book call for T-1-11 exterior siding. This material is very similar to plywood and is sold in the same dimensions. The major difference between plywood and T-1-11 exterior siding is that the latter has a slightly grooved surface.

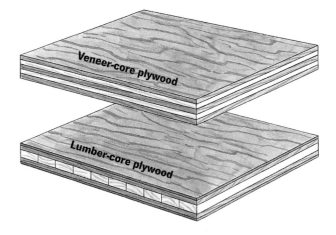

DOWELS

The sunshade featured on page 114 requires dowels. These are round, wooden rods that come in diameters ranging from $\frac{1}{8}$ inch to $1\frac{1}{4}$ inches, and are available in 36-inch and 48-inch lengths. You can find dowels at any hardware and building-supply store.

BUYING LUMBER

A few minutes of preparation before shopping for materials can save you hours of time. Start by making a complete list of what you need to build your project. Look at the Cutting List that accompanies each project to determine how much lumber to buy and in what dimensions. Consider your mode of transportation, too. Long boards may not fit into a small car, so if you don't own a pickup truck, you may want to borrow one.

Although we've recommended specific kinds of wood for each project, you should feel free to substitute another kind of lumber that may be more readily available. Before making a substitution, however, check with independent lumberyards or mills in your area; they often carry specialty woods—such as cedar in dimensions thicker than 1 x—that you usually can't find at chain stores or large home-improvement centers.

If at all possible, inspect each board before handing over any money. When you purchase wood for a particular project, hold boards of the same nominal dimension against each other to make certain that they are all exactly the same thickness and width. Because most lumberyards have more than one supplier, boards in the same bin—with the same stated nominal dimensions—may vary slightly; a $\frac{1}{64}$-inch variation may not seem like a big deal, but it can be just enough to ensure that your project won't fit together correctly.

Check for all the defects described and illustrated on page 12, too. Although the better grades of lumber should be free from major defects, a few minutes spent

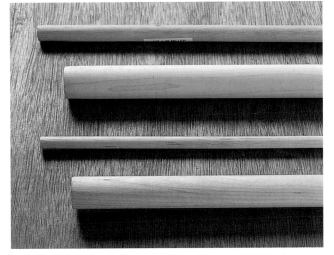

Dowels

inspecting each piece before buying can save you a lot of time and wasted wood down the road. A few more minutes spent neatly restacking the lumber that's left will ensure that your local lumberyard will allow you (and other customers) to continue this kind of "hand-picking."

Keep the project's Cutting List in mind as you select lumber. If your project requires only very short pieces, you may be able to buy a less expensive, lower grade of lumber; however, if you're building something made from very long pieces, find the straightest, clearest lumber possible.

The Cutting List will also help you choose the right lengths to buy your lumber in. For instance, a project may require twenty-four linear feet of 2 x 4 cedar or pine. You could buy that quantity in four six-foot pieces or in three eight-foot pieces; however, if the Cutting List calls for seven-foot pieces, you'll obviously want to buy your lumber in eight-foot lengths.

Finally, overbuying lumber is never a bad idea. We've allowed for a slight overage in the amount of lumber called for in the Materials List that accompanies each project; however, you'll never regret having extra boards on hand—especially if it saves you running back to the lumberyard for "just one more 2 x 4."

TOOL BOX

▼BASIC TOOLS

- Smooth, level work surface
- Shop rags
- Safety glasses, dust mask, and earplugs
- Tape measure, straight edge, combination square, compass, protractor, pencil, and utility knife
- Claw hammer, tack hammer, and nail set
- Assortment of Phillips-head screwdrivers
- Power drill and a variety of bits, including combination countersink and pilot bits
- Quick-grip clamps, bar or pipe clamps, and C-clamps—at least two of each type
- Combination saw, or ripsaw and crosscut saw, and coping saw
- Sanding block and sandpapers ranging from coarse to fine
- Variety of chisels, rasps, and files

▼OPTIONAL TOOLS

- Circular saw with rip fence, and jigsaw
- Orbital palm-sander or belt-sander
- Router and a variety of bits
- Low-angle block plane and jackplane

TOOLS AND TECHNIQUES

Most woodworkers start out with just a few tools and limited expertise. With time, they add to their stock of each. If you're just starting out, there's no need to go broke equipping your shop (or that small corner of the basement that you hope will someday grow into a shop) with every tool that's mentioned below. Start with the basics listed in the Tool Box to the left. Then scan the list of Additional Tool(s) that accompanies the project you plan to build. Rent what you don't own, and add a new tool or two each time you build a new project.

When you do make a tool purchase, always buy the best product you can afford. High-quality equipment may not turn you into an expert woodworker, but at least it will still be around after you've become one.

Although we've given general tips for using each tool that's described in this section, manufacturers have an interest in making sure that you know how to use their products, so their instructional information can be a great resource. Be sure to read and keep any warranty and operation and maintenance material that comes with your tools. If you're still not sure exactly how a tool should work, ask a friend who has a lot of woodworking experience (and who isn't missing any fingers), take a trip to the library, or consult with a salesperson at your local hardware store. Most folks are happy to share their knowledge.

YOUR WORK SPACE

You don't need a huge, extravagantly equipped workshop to build beautiful wood projects. What you do need is a safe and comfortable space where you'll be able to focus on your work. Stake out an area that's dry, well lit, and well ventilated. Check the wiring to make sure it's adequate to handle the electrical demands of your power tools.

When you've found and claimed your work space, establish a system for keeping your tools organized and in tip-top condition. Store them where they're handy for you, but safe from rust, dings, children, and other potential hazards.

WORKBENCH

The first "tool" to install in your shop is a workbench. This can be any steady, level work surface. It's where you'll do everything from marking and measuring to clamping and cutting. Position your workbench so that you can approach it from all sides. Your bench should be hip height and very solid; if it's not completely stable, fasten it to the floor.

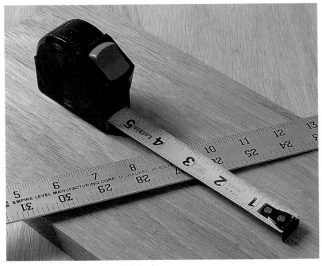

Tape measure and straightedge

MEASURING

If you've spent much time with an experienced wood-worker, you've probably heard the sayings "Don't cut until you must" and "Measure twice, cut once." A corollary to both of these hallowed woodworking axioms is: "If possible, measure against the fit." In other words, hold the board to be cut against the place where the piece will fit; then adjust the measurements as necessary. There's a reason that the best woodworkers utter all three of these sayings: Careful and accurate measurement and marking form the foundation of successful woodworking. The correct layout of lengths, joints, and angles all determine how well the finished project will fit together. So choose the correct measuring tools for your job and make good use of them.

STEEL TAPE MEASURE

This flexible "roll-up" ruler extends from inside a compact case and secures to the end of your work by means of a hook that's mounted loosely to compensate for its own thickness. The first 12 inches of a tape measure are marked in $\frac{1}{32}$-inch increments; after that, the graduations are marked in $\frac{1}{16}$-inch increments. A $\frac{3}{4}$-inch-wide, 16-foot-long, self-retracting rule with a tape-lock button and belt clip will serve you well for all of the projects in this book.

STRAIGHTEDGE

This tool is simply a steel ruler, between 12 inches and 36 inches long. Use it to mark straight lines and to make close measurements. Protect your straightedge's smooth edges from nicks by storing it well away from other metal objects.

TRY SQUARE

This handy tool consists of a metal blade placed at a right angle to a metal, plastic, or wooden handle. You'll use a try square to establish a 90° angle; it can also be used to mark cuts across the face of a board and to transfer lines to all three sides of a board. Larger try squares (16 inches and up) are called framing squares.

Framing square, try square, and combination square

COMBINATION SQUARE

This versatile tool consists of a cast handle fitted to a metal blade. The handle can be moved back and forth perpendicular to the blade and is designed in such a way that it also forms a 45° angle with the blade. The blade is marked in ¹⁄₁₆-inch gradations for close measurements. In addition to doing everything a try square does, the combination square measures 45° angles and can act as a depth and miter gauge.

SLIDING T-BEVEL

With its wooden handle and adjustable metal blade, this tool is the standard for establishing angles. The blade swivels and slides within the handle and can be locked at any position; it does not, however, provide a reading of the angle itself. You'll use this tool primarily to check and transfer bevels (page 27) and mitered ends (page 27).

PROTRACTOR

This half-moon-shaped tool allows you to mark any angle from 0° to 180°. It can also be used to transfer angles from an existing joint to another location.

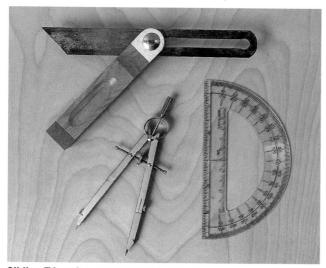

Sliding T-bevel, compass, and protractor

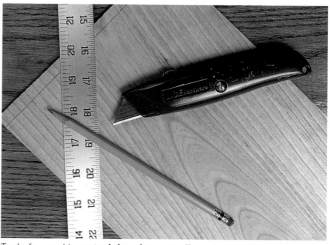

Tools for marking: **straight edge, pencil, and utility knife**

COMPASS

A compass has two legs; one ends in a point that acts as a pivot, and the other holds a pencil. You'll use a compass to scribe and transfer arcs, circles, and patterns.

PENCIL AND UTILITY KNIFE

Careful marking goes hand in hand with careful measuring. A pencil will work fine for most jobs, but pencil marks don't always show on dark or damp wood; a line scribed with a sharp blade will. The best utility knives have retractable blades and a blade storage pocket built right into the handle.

Whether you use a well-sharpened pencil or a utility knife, mark points with a small V on the waste side of the line; the point of the V will show you exactly where to cut.

CLAMPING

Whether you're measuring, marking, drilling, or cutting, you'll need a steady hand and a steady piece of wood. A little less coffee might help with the first part, but clamps are a sure bet for the second! You'll use these tools to grip parts together or to a bench to keep them from shifting as you work. You'll also use them to hold together glued pieces while the glue dries. Combining clamps with strips of wood can extend the tool's grip over a larger area, and can also form improvised saw- and router-guides. Clamps can leave marks on your work, so be sure to sandwich scrap wood between the clamp ends and your project.

Clamps come in a variety of styles and sizes, some of which are described below. Don't be alarmed—you won't need every one of these! A selection of quick-grip, C-, and bar or pipe clamps should give you ample holding power for the projects in this book. Just be sure to have several of whichever type you select because you'll need pairs of clamps to apply pressure evenly over large pieces of work. For the best results with any of type of clamp, tighten the tools until they're snug, but not too tight. Also, when piece- or joint-clamping, place the tool's pressure point directly at the center line of the work or the joint to be glued.

C-CLAMPS

As their name suggests, these tools are formed in the shape of the letter C. One end of the C is fixed; the other end opens and closes by means of a threaded rod and swivel pad that can be fastened securely across an

Clockwise from top: **C-clamps, quick-grip clamp, and spring clamps**

opening. Use C-clamps to hold together joints and thicknesses of wood, or to secure wood to a work surface. They're inexpensive and versatile, so you'll probably want to buy C-clamps in a variety of sizes.

SPRING CLAMPS

Spring clamps will perform many of the same functions as C-clamps, but on a smaller scale; a 3-inch maximum opening is the largest size commonly available.

QUICK-GRIP CLAMPS

Similar in appearance and function to bar clamps (see below), quick-grip clamps tighten by means of a trigger rather than by a threaded rod screw. The trigger permits one-handed operation, which makes the tool especially useful for beginning woodworkers.

PIPE CLAMPS AND BAR CLAMPS

Pipe clamps and bar clamps are excellent for spanning and securing long or very wide pieces of wood. They can also grip together boards placed edge to edge (see edge-to-edge joint illustration on page 26). Their frames consist of sections of iron plumbing pipe (pipe clamps) or lengths of steel or aluminum bars (bar clamps). A fixed head with a short, threaded rod and a metal pad is mounted on one end of the frame. At the other end is a sliding tail stop that can be locked anywhere along the frame's length to accommodate the work. Bar clamps are more effective than pipe clamps, but they're also more expensive.

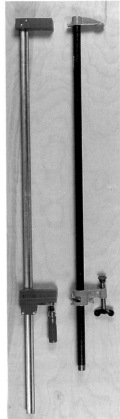

Bar clamp and pipe clamp

CUTTING

Different saws do different things. Some saws are designed for cutting across a wood's grain; others are designed for cutting with or along the grain. Some saws make quick, rough cuts, and others make slow, fine cuts. How do you determine which saw is right for your job? It's all in the teeth. The more and smaller teeth a saw has (a measurement given in points per inch), the smoother and slower a cut it will make. Fewer and larger teeth will result in a quicker, coarser cut. The pitch, bevel, and angle of the teeth will all affect a saw's function, too.

Always check to make sure that your saws' blades are sharp and well maintained. Between uses, protect your handsaws by slipping a length of slit garden hose over their blades' cutting edges. Keep the blades of power saws in tip-top condition by hanging them from a peg board, rather than tossing them into a drawer where they'll bang into one another. When saw blades do become dull, an experienced saw-sharpener can return their edges in just a few minutes.

Keep in mind that every saw will remove an amount of wood from the piece you are cutting equal to the thickness of its blade. This waste is called a saw's kerf, and you'll need to account for it whenever you make a cut.

Handsaw

HANDSAWS

With a few exceptions (noted in the directions) you can make all of the cuts necessary for the projects in this book with saws powered by nothing more than your own muscle. Just keep in mind that cutting with handsaws requires some extra time and patience.

Crosscut Saw

A crosscut saw is used to cut across or against the wood's grain. For instance, if you need to cut a 6-foot-long 2 x 4 down to a length of 5½ feet, this tool will do the job.

When you make the cut, grip the saw firmly with the ball of your palm fitted against the back of the handle. Be sure to cut on the waste edge of the cutting line; try to remove just half of the pencil or blade line. For the best results, hold the blade at a 45° angle. Start the cut by pulling backwards on the saw, while guiding the teeth with the outer edge of your thumb. This will make an indentation that holds the saw blade in place while you continue. Then, keeping your shoulder, arm, and hand parallel to the blade throughout the cutting process, cut by applying pressure only on the downstrokes.

Ripsaw

A ripsaw cuts (or rips) with or along the wood's grain. It's what you'd use to rip a strip 3 inches wide and 12 inches long from a piece that's 5½ inches wide and 12 inches long. Use the same technique for ripping as for crosscutting, but hold the blade at a 60° angle. In a pinch, a crosscut saw can rip, but a ripsaw should never be used for making crosscuts.

Coping Saw

This saw consists of a steel, U-shaped frame with a very thin, brittle blade fastened under tension across the U's opening (see the photo on page 22). A handle is attached to the frame for ease of sawing. The blade has between 10 and 12 teeth per inch and makes fine, smooth cuts.

Use a coping saw to make curved and interior cuts on wood less than 2 inches thick. The saw's frame can be angled away from the blade for cutting curved cut-lines, and the blade can be unfastened, slipped through an opening in the work, and refastened to cut out interior shapes. Mount the blade so that the teeth point toward the handle; this way, it will cut on the upstroke. Then use a light touch and a smooth sawing action.

Backsaw and Miter Box

A backsaw has an 8-inch- to 12-inch-long rectangular blade stretched between the points of an elongated, U-shaped frame. A reinforcing strip of thicker metal bent around the back of the blade prevents it from flexing. The blade, which is often used to make smooth joinery cuts, generally has about 15 points per inch.

Backsaws are often used with a miter box, a box that's open at both ends, with slotted sides to guide a saw in cutting joints. Standard miter boxes are built for making 45°- and 90°-angle cuts. Better-quality boxes come with saws that fit in a special jig and can be adjusted to cut any angle from 45° to 90°.

POWER SAWS

Unless you have hours and hours of free time, you'll probably want to use a power saw for at least some of your cutting jobs. If the thought of buying power equipment sends your wallet into shock, but you don't have time to work with handsaws, consider renting for the weekend. Be sure to thoroughly check all tools before leaving the store, though; rental equipment can take a beating, and you should be sure that you've rented a tool that's safe and in good shape.

Circular Saws and Fences

Possibly the most popular power tool in existence, the circular saw can make short work of most cutting jobs. Its round, 7¼-inch blade can be adjusted to cut angles from 45° to 90°. Set to perpendicular, the blade will penetrate to a depth of 2¼ inches; that depth is reduced to 1¾ inches at the 45°-angle setting.

Circular saw with ripfence fitted into the base plate

Circular saws do have their drawbacks. They're heavy, and they can be a little unwieldy—factors that make for less-than-accurate cuts; however, a fence, a tool used as a guide for performing various cutting and boring tasks, can dramatically improve your accuracy with this tool. If you use your circular saw for rip cutting, you'll want a rip fence. The ideal rip fence fits into the base plate of the saw itself and adjusts for the width to be ripped.

If you're not comfortable with a circular saw, put in some practice

Backsaw and miter box

time with scrap wood before using it on high-quality lumber. When you're ready to start work, adjust the saw's blade depth so that the teeth will penetrate the wood fully. To adjust the depth, check the manual that comes with the saw you have; you'll probably need to loosen a lever or knob and move the shoe up and down. Make sure that the work to be cut is clamped securely in place and that the tool's cord is behind you. Don your safety glasses and earplugs. Check to make sure that nothing other than the work itself is in the path of the cut, above or below the work. Sight your cut line along the mark on the front of the saw's shoe, grip the saw firmly, but not tensely, and start your cut.

Jigsaw (or Saber Saw)

The power answer to a coping saw, this tool has a narrow reciprocating blade perfect for cutting curves and interior shapes in wood up to 1½ inches thick. The "shoe" that surrounds the blade can be adjusted to allow cuts at any angle between 45° and 90°. Jigsaw blades are available with various numbers of points per inch. Blades with fewer points per inch will cut tighter circles than those with more points per inch.

Better-quality jigsaws have a variable speed control and orbital blade

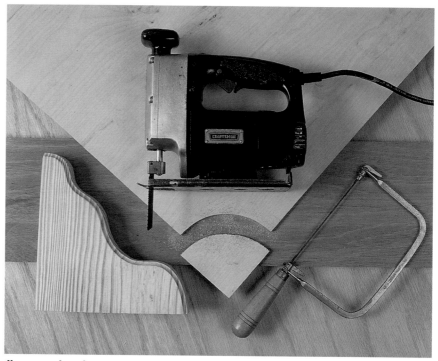

Jigsaw and coping saw

action; this action swings the blade's cutting edge forward into the work and back again, through the blade's up and down cycle. A blower clears the sawdust to keep the cutting line clear.

SHAPING, SMOOTHING, FILLING, AND SANDING

You'll enjoy your project much more if it's attractively shaped, smooth, and splinter-free. Aside from esthetics and your personal comfort, wood must have a smooth, even surface before it receives its first coat of sealer, stain, or paint. Rasps and files will round edges and remove excess material. Chisels and mallets

are used to cut and clean joints. Routers can add interesting design elements and perform the work of several hand tools. Planes level wood and ready it for sanding. Use a wood filler to cover small nail and screw holes. Sandpaper completes the job by smoothing the project to a fine finish.

RASPS AND FILES

Smooth, rounded edges on wooden projects can be achieved with rasps and files. These shaping tools have metal blades that are textured on at least one side. Use a wood rasp to make the first cut in removing wood stock for shaping or rounding; then make finer cuts with a cabinet rasp.

Both tools are typically 10 inches long and available in three styles: flat on both sides, half-round, and round.

Wood files are similar to rasps, but are used for finer cuts and general smoothing. They're usually about 10 inches long, and come in many shapes, including half-round and round styles.

Planes

Files and rasps

Chisels and mallet

CHISELS AND MALLETS

Cleaning up joints and hollowing out sections of wood are jobs best done with a chisel and a mallet. These simple tools have wooden or plastic handles attached to flat blades that are bevelled on the top and very flat on the bottom. Spend a little extra money to get good chisels; the extra dollars will translate into blades that will hold their edges and stay sharper longer. Look for chisels with reinforced plastic handles that can withstand use with a mallet.

Unless you're paring very small, easily removed bits of wood, you'll use a mallet to provide force on the chisel. Strike the chisel's handle lightly to avoid gouging the wood or taking big bites. When using a chisel without a mallet, hold the tool at a slight downward angle with one hand to provide the force, and guide it with the other.

PLANES

Planes are used to surface and smooth wood. They come in a variety of sizes and styles to perform a variety of jobs, but they all function in basically the same way. The working part of the tool consists of a frog that adjusts backwards and forwards to narrow the tool's mouth for finer work and to widen it for rougher work. A blade called an iron performs the actual cutting. A knob connected to a screw mechanism that runs parallel to the length of the iron adjusts that piece to control the depth of cuts. On all but block planes, a chip breaker fits over the blade and breaks the wood shavings as they come through the plane's mouth. On some planes, a wedge iron caps the chip breaker and holds all of the working pieces together; this whole ensemble sits on top of a flat, sometimes corrugated sole that has a small mouth through which the cutting iron is exposed. The front of the plane has a round knob that you'll grasp to help guide the tool, and the back has a handle that you'll hold as you push the tool over the work.

Two basic planes will perform all the planing work necessary for the projects in this book: a 14-inch jack-plane and a 6-inch, low-angle block plane. Use the jackplane for general surfacing and the block plane for trimming end grain.

For work with either type of plane, begin by sharpening the iron. For general work, it should be barely above the sole (as viewed from the flat, or sole side of the tool), and just visible for fine work. For general surfacing, stand directly behind the piece you're working, inner foot slightly back and outer foot forward. Apply pressure to the front of the plane as you begin the stroke; then shift pressure to the back as you finish. Always plane with the grain of the wood, which can switch directions several times on the same board. If the wood tears out, rather than cutting smoothly, you're planing against the grain.

Successful hand planing requires time, strength, patience—and tools with flawlessly sharp blades. Keep your planes in top condition by cleaning your work of any debris before planing; dirt and grit will dull a blade quickly. When you're finished, store the tool on its side.

ROUTER

A router is a hand-held power tool that can cut decorative shapes and round edges, create grooves and

Router, router bits, and wrenches

notches, and make joints (pages 26–27). The tool has a round baseplate that adjusts up and down to control the cutting depth. The baseplate supports a motor, on the shaft of which a collet is mounted. A cutting bit fits into the collet and protrudes from an opening in the center of the baseplate. To change the shape of a cut, simply use a bit that produces the pattern you want.

Routers can be difficult to operate, so put in plenty of practice time on scrap wood before using these tools on serious work.

WOOD FILLER AND PLUGS

The easiest way to cover screw holes and nail holes in woodwork is to use wood filler, a colored plastic substance that hardens when exposed to air. There are also wax-based filling sticks that are particularly useful for hiding small nail holes. When selecting a color of either the plastic- or wax-based filler, visualize how the wood will look after it's finished and try to match the filler to that color. Follow the manufacturer's instructions for use.

Plugs offer another option for filling screw holes. To cut custom plugs, you need a drill press—an advanced power tool that's not described in this book. However, you can often order ready-made plugs made from the wood you're using. To use a plug, bore a $3/16$-inch-deep counter-sink hole (see page 29) with the same diameter as the plug. Dip the plug in a small puddle of glue, start it into its hole, and tap it into place with a hammer. Allow the glue to cure; then trim it with a sharp chisel or a low-angle block plane.

SANDPAPER

The final step in readying a project for finishing is sanding, and the first step in sanding is selecting the correct grade of sandpaper. Sandpaper is available in several grits, or grades of coarseness. The common grits are: coarse (No. 60), medium (No. 100), fine (No. 150), and extra-fine (No. 220). Most stores carry other grits as well.

Palm orbital sanders, sand paper for orbital sanders, sanding block, and sandpaper

Start with a grade coarse enough to efficiently remove all defects from the surface except for the scratches that the sandpaper makes. Usually 100-grit paper is a good place to start. Because you have removed all blemishes with the first grit you use, each succeeding grit (150 and 220, or 120, 150, 180, and 220) must remove only the scratches from the previous sandpaper. Don't jump ahead, figuring that the marks or scratches will magically disappear under later sanding grits or under your finish. Only paint will hide these blemishes; clear finishes always make them more apparent.

SANDING BLOCK

This is a small, hand-held block with a flat bottom and clips on either end for holding sandpaper in place. Although using a sanding block is more time consuming than working with a power sander, it will get the job done. Even if you start with a power sander, you should do the final finishing work with an easy-to-control sanding block.

BELT AND PALM (OR PAD) ORBITAL SANDERS

These are the most common hand-held power sanding tools. A belt sander makes use of a continually moving belt of sandpaper. Good for general surfacing, a belt sander is also powerful enough to remove dents and tool marks in wood. Simply float the tool back and forth across the work, holding it with both hands and following the grain of the wood. Always handle this powerful sander with a firm but light touch; it works very quickly and can remove too much wood if you're not careful.

Light-weight and designed for one-handed operation, palm (or pad) orbital sanders have a flat pad to which a piece of sandpaper attaches by means of hook-and-loop tape or mechanical clips. Some palm sanders have round pads that spin. Other orbital sanders have rectangular pads that vibrate back and forth.

STATIONARY POWER TOOLS

Although they offer greater accuracy and more sophisticated cutting options than hand-held tools, stationary power tools are not for the beginner, and none of the projects in this book requires them. If you'd like to learn how to use stationary power tools, ask an expert to introduce you to their safe use, or take a class at a local school or a community college. And, as with any tool, read the manufacturer's instructions for operation, use, and maintenance.

JOINTS, CUTS, AND JOINERY

Woodworkers use hundreds of different methods to join together pieces of wood. These unions can be as simple as an end butted up against an edge and held with nails or screws, or as complex as hand cut-pegs, shaped to fit into custom-cut slots. The projects in this book use the simpler methods of joinery. With experience, however, you may find that you'd like to try some of the more complex techniques. No matter what kind of joinery you try, remember not to use glue on end grain; it simply will not hold.

BUTT JOINT▲

In this simplest, but weakest of all joints, one board abuts another at a right angle. Nails or screws hold the pieces together.

EDGE-TO-EDGE JOINT▼

This joint creates a wider piece of wood from several narrow pieces by joining them together edge to edge. Start by ripping a very small strip from the edges of the boards to be joined; this will guarantee a perfect fit. Apply glue to each adjoining edge; then use bar or pipe clamps to apply firm, even pressure along the length of the piece, alternating the clamps above and below. If all of the glue squeezes out, or if the glued piece bows across its width, you have applied too much pressure; loosen the clamps slightly.

For very long edge joints, place extra boards above and below, across the width of the piece; then secure them with C-clamps. Keep the clamping boards from becoming glued to the work piece by putting a piece of waxed paper or plastic between the two.

BEVEL CUTS▲

A bevel is an angular cut that produces a new surface on the board. It's simply a surface at any angle other than 90° to any of its neighbors.

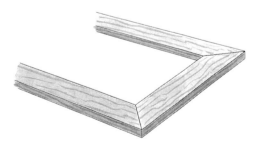

MITER CUTS AND JOINTS▼

A miter is an angle, usually 45°, cut perpendicularly across the width of a board. Two mitered or beveled boards joined together to create a right angle without exposing the end grain of either piece form a miter joint. This joint's fit depends entirely on how well you measure the angles before cutting, so measure carefully. Because glue does not hold end grain, miter joints are weak and must be reinforced with screws or nails.

DADO CUTS AND JOINTS►

A dado is a slot or a groove cut into the face of a board. To form a dado joint, fit the thickness of another board into the slot; then secure it with glue and screws or nails. You can cut a dado with a handsaw and a chisel, or with a router. The illustration to the right shows one technique for cutting a dado.

HALF-LAP JOINT▼

This joint connects two pieces of wood that are equal in thickness by interlocking and overlapping them. The portable sunshade on page 114 uses half–lap joints. A dado is cut in each piece, one-half the thickness of the wood. Then the pieces of wood are fit together at the notches, and their faces are flush when the joint is complete.

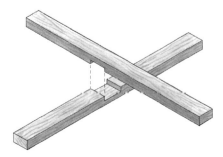

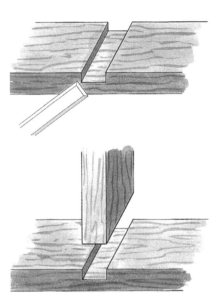

FASTENING

The fasteners you choose for the projects in this book should be able to withstand the rigors of the great outdoors. Hot-dipped, galvanized steel nails and screws provide good weather-resistance at a relatively low cost; however, if you don't mind spending the extra money, fasteners made from stainless steel will outlast any other kind on the market.

When you're selecting fasteners, consider the material they'll be joining. You may not want to spend the extra money on stainless-steel screws if you're working with inexpensive pine. On the other hand, galvanized metal can stain cedar, so stainless steel may be worth a few more dollars per project.

Claw hammers, nail set, and finishing nails

NAILS AND BRADS

Nails are categorized according to their use and their size. Nails used for construction and other rough work are called common. You won't use them very often in woodworking. Instead, you'll reach for finishing nails, ring-shank nails, or spiral nails.

Finishing nails are cut from wire and they have very small heads that virtually disappear into the work. Ring shank nails (sometimes called annular-ring nails) have sharp-edged rings on their shanks that allow them to hold tighter than common nails. Spiral nails have spiraled shanks.

They turn like screws when you drive them into wood, offering a tight hold.

The garden bench on page 119 calls for timber spikes (sometimes called pole-barn nails). These are very long nails with slightly spiraled shanks.

Most nails are named according to the penny system; this system derives its name from the antiquated English penny, which is represented by the letter "d". Originally, the system designated the price of nails per 100 of a given type; today, it designates the length of a nail. Nails range in length from 1 inch to 6 inches, and they increase in diameter as their length increases. The table above and to the right shows the most common length of nails and their penny sizes.

Brads are the exception to the penny-system rule. These small, thin versions of finishing nails are named according to their wire gauge, ranging from 11 to 20, and by their length in inches. You'll use brads on very small projects or to attach trim.

The thicknesses of the two pieces of wood that you're joining will determine the size of nail you need. Select a nail that will penetrate the second thickness of wood as far as possible without coming through its opposite surface.

If you're working with hardwood or a softwood that has a tendency to

Length (in.)	Penny Size
1	2d
$1\frac{1}{4}$	3d
$1\frac{1}{2}$	4d
$1\frac{3}{4}$	5d
2	6d
$2\frac{1}{4}$	7d
$2\frac{1}{2}$	8d
$2\frac{3}{4}$	9d
3	10d
$3\frac{1}{4}$	12d
$3\frac{1}{2}$	16d
4	20d

split when nailed, pre-drill holes for the nails. These holes are called pilot holes. Make them about two-thirds the length of the nail and slightly smaller in diameter.

Driving nails at an angle, rather than straight in, produces an even tighter hold; this process is known as toenailing (see the illustration below). To toenail, clamp the pieces in place and bore a pilot hole. Use a hammer to tap the nail into the wood until only the head and a small portion of the shank show above the wood. Then use a tool called a nail set (described below) to countersink the head.

NAIL SET

This is a simple metal tool with a narrow point on one end and a flat face on the other. It's used to sink nails below the surface, a process called countersinking, without leaving hammer marks on the wood. Place the narrow end against the head of the nail and tap the tool's other end with a hammer.

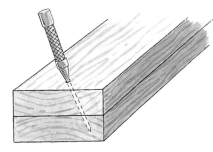

HAMMERS

A 16-ounce claw hammer and a 6-ounce tack hammer will serve your hammering needs for most of the projects in this book.

SCREWS

You'll ask for screws by their length and the diameter of their shank. The chart above and to the right shows the most common screw sizes.

As with nails, use screws that penetrate the second thickness of wood as far as possible without coming through its opposite surface. You'll also need to select screws in a diameter that won't split the wood.

Screw Chart

Gauge No.	4	6	8	10	12
Shank Diameter	$7/64$"	$9/64$"	$5/32$"	$3/16$"	$7/32$"
Lengths	$3/8$"–1"	$1/2$"–2"	$1/2$"–3"	$3/4$"–$3 1/2$"	$3/4$"–$3 1/2$"

Although several types of screws are available, we recommend exterior decking screws with either a Phillips-head or square-recess flathead; both head types are equally suitable, so use whichever is convenient. Either type can be easily countersunk, and, like all decking screws, they're specifically designed for outdoor use.

PILOT HOLES

When using screws, always bore a pilot hole first using a power drill. Technically, this hole can consist of up to three parts: the pilot, or lead hole, which should be about half the diameter of the screw; the shank hole, which should be the same diameter as the screw's shank; and the countersink or bore, into which the screw head should fit.

A simple lead hole, bored to about half the screw's length, is sufficient for most softwoods. A full-length pilot hole and shank hole are only necessary for very long screws or for screw holes in extremely dense hardwoods. You'll use what's known as a combination countersink and pilot bit to bore pilot holes, and this will automatically create the countersink.

SCREWDRIVERS

If you're working with a very soft wood, you may be able to drive in screws with nothing more than a hand screwdriver. As long as you're using Phillips-head screws, a simple No. 2 Phillips-head screwdriver will work well for the projects in this book.

Screws and Phillips-head screwdrivers

Drills and assorted drill bits

DRILLS

If there's one power tool you should think about buying, it's a power drill. These tools come in several varieties with an endless assortment of interchangeable bits that will allow the same tool to bore holes and drive screws of many different sizes and styles. The most popular and versatile of these are electric variable-speed, reversible drills. Start your collection of power woodworking tools with a drill with a $\frac{3}{8}$-inch chuck capacity and at least a 3.5-amp motor. The variable-speed control will allow you to adjust the drill's motor speed to accommodate several kinds of work, and the reversible motor makes removing screws just as easy as inserting them.

Improvements in technology have made today's light-weight cordless drills as convenient and versatile as the heavier plug-in varieties. Most have a clutch, which makes driving screws much easier because the drill can stop itself when the screw snugs up.

Drill Bits

You'll find a bit for just about every kind of hole you need to drill and for every screw you need to drive. Combination countersink and pilot bits, made for screw sizes Nos. 4–12, bore the pilot hole and the sink for screw holes at the same time; these are your best choice for boring pilot holes, particularly if you use the same size screw on a regular basis. Spade bits are designed with a flat cutting edge on either side of a center point to bore quick, clean holes; they're available in $\frac{1}{4}$-inch to $1\frac{1}{2}$-inch diameters. Brad-point bits will leave a clean, smooth-sided hole for $\frac{1}{8}$-inch- to $\frac{1}{2}$-inch-diameter screws. Power-drive bits turn a power drill into an excellent substitute for handheld screwdrivers; these useful bits slip onto a drill's chuck by means of a short, six-sided shank, and are available for Phillips-head, slotted, and, increasingly, square-recess-head screws.

Depth-Control Stop Collars

You'll use these metal rings to control the depth of a bit's penetration. They fit around drill bits' shafts and can be locked at any point. Stop collars are available in sizes to fit bit diameters from $\frac{1}{8}$ inch to $\frac{1}{2}$ inch.

BOLTS AND WRENCHES

Bolts are the strongest fasteners of all. Use them with nuts and flat washers to secure joints and large structural pieces. They're available in lengths from $\frac{3}{4}$ inch to 5 inches, and in diameters from $\frac{1}{4}$ inch to $\frac{5}{8}$ inch.

Before inserting bolts in wood, bore a through-hole. To do this without splintering the wood, clamp a piece of scrap wood to the back of the piece through which you're boring the hole. Then bore the hole all the way through the scrap.

The projects in this book that require bolts call for either lag bolts (sometimes referred to as lag screws) or carriage bolts. Lag bolts are actually heavy-duty wood screws with square or hexagonal heads. To tighten a lag bolt, grip the head and turn the bolt with a wrench. An 8-inch adjustable wrench is the best choice for this job. With its knurled thumbwheel that controls and locks the wrench jaws, this tool will accommodate a $^3/_{16}$-inch-faced to 1-inch-faced hex or square nut.

Carriage bolts have unslotted, oval heads and a square shoulder that sinks into the wood to prevent turning. After you've inserted a carriage bolt in the through hole, tap its head with a hammer to drive the square shoulder into the wood.

GLUES AND ADHESIVES

The projects in this book are destined for outdoor use, so a weatherproof adhesive is essential any time that glue is required. Look for the outdoor formulation of ordinary carpenter's glue; it will be labeled "for exterior

Paint brushes, foam brushes, and assorted finishes

use." Not only will this glue hold up against moisture and the other dangers of outdoor life, it will also set in less than 45 minutes and cure in less than a day's time. If you can't find it, use the more costly two-part resorcinol; follow the manufacturer's instructions, and keep in mind that it will take at least 12 hours to set and another 12 hours to cure properly.

Use a light touch when applying glue. Start by running a thin ribbon of adhesive down the center of one of the pieces to be glued. Rub the adjoining surface against the ribbon to distribute the glue In a thin, even coat over both surfaces; then clamp

the pieces together. A little extra glue should squeeze out from the joint. Let this excess dry completely; then trim it with a chisel or low angle block plane and sand off any remaining residue.

FINISHING

Finishing is the final step before putting a project out into the garden for years of enjoyment. In fact, proper finishing can add to those years substantially. Even projects made from pressure-treated wood or naturally weather-resistant cedar or redwood will benefit from a coat or two of paint or an application of sealer.

The type of lumber you use will more or less determine the kind of finish you choose. You'll almost certainly want to paint a project made from a lower grade of softwood or pressure-treated lumber; the opaque finish will cover any imperfections and can turn an inexpensive project into a beautiful showpiece. On the other hand, if you spent the extra money for naturally beautiful redwood, a simple coat of clear sealer will give the project added protection without covering the wood's attractive grain.

Choose a well-ventilated area for applying finishes, and protect your work surface with a layer of newspaper. Make sure the project is sanded to a smooth finish and is completely clean and dry. Each type and brand of finish varies slightly, so always read the manufacturer's instructions; they'll tell you how long the finish will take to dry and whether or not a second or third coat is needed. They may also recommend a preferred type of applicator. If not, just use a good quality, synthetic brush made from nylon or polyester; inexpensive, disposable foam brushes offer another good option.

All finishes are available in latex (or water-based) and alkyd (the modern equivalent of oil-based) formulations. Latex finishes are easier to apply and dry much faster, but alkyds last longer and offer a greater degree of protection.

WATER SEALER

Most water sealers available today are "penetrating finishes," meaning that they penetrate the surface of the wood and offer a high degree of protection. Sealers will have the least effect on your wood's appearance. They're often used to weatherproof decks and railings, and are a good choice for outdoor projects made from attractive woods. Water sealers range in appearance from muted and barely perceptible to smooth and semi-gloss sheens. Be sure to buy a finish sealer rather than a clear sanding sealer. Plan to reapply water sealers every year.

STAINS

Stains come in a huge variety of colors and styles, ranging from almost translucent to nearly opaque. Many are also available in penetrating formulations and contain a sealer; these are the best choice for outdoor projects. (Stains that don't contain a sealer won't offer protection from the elements.) Stains don't require a primer of any kind, and one coat usually offers sufficient protection against water damage. You should reapply stains every two to three years.

PAINTS

Whether your taste runs toward modest beige or electric purple, there's a paint out there to suit your needs. If you don't see it on the shelf, you can have a color custom mixed. Keep in mind, though, that the color shown on the can may not look exactly the same once it's applied to your project. Choose among high-gloss enamels, flat-sheen paints with a more matte finish, and several styles in between.

All paints require a primer, too. This essential base coat will seal the wood's surface and aid in the paint's adhesion. Be sure to match the primer and paint types; you must use a latex primer with latex paint and an alkyd primer with alkyd paint.

Before you make your paint purchase, check to be sure you're buying an exterior-grade product. Look for a warranty, too; this will tell you approximately how many years the paint will last. Finally, don't leave the store without a couple of stirring sticks; the pigment in paint tends to settle, and you'll need to gently remix it if it sits for any length of time.

BEFORE YOU GET STARTED

Take a few minutes to read this section! In it, we explain exactly how the project instructions are organized, and we offer some tips that will make building your project go much more smoothly.

SELECTING A PROJECT

You've probably already browsed through the pages of this book and found several projects you'd like to build. Before you run out to buy a load of lumber, though, take a few more minutes to narrow your choices down to the first project you want to tackle. For many people, the process of woodworking is reward enough in itself. But it's also nice to end up with something you'd like to keep or would be proud to give as a gift.

If you're building something for yourself, consider where you want to put it. Maybe you love the arbor-bench combination on page 56; it's a big project, though, so you'll want to make sure you have ample room for it before you spend the time and money to build it. If you're building something as a gift, keep the intended gift-receiver's space restraints in mind, too.

Next, take a look at the lists of materials, tools, and hardware required to build your chosen project. Will you need to buy or rent a special tool? How much will the lumber cost? Try to evaluate about how much the project will cost to build *before* you begin construction.

Then read the directions all the way through to determine the amount of time you'll need to build the project. See if the construction

An Aside About Lumber

Throughout this book, you'll see the parts of boards referred to by specific names. The long, width surfaces are called edges; the short width surfaces are the ends; and the broad, length surfaces are known as a board's faces.

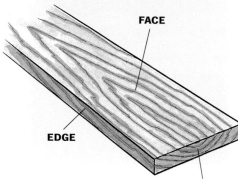

FACE

EDGE

END

requires any techniques that you're not comfortable with; if it does, take some time to review those techniques in the Woodworking Basics chapter, or—if necessary—in a basic woodworking-techniques book or with a woodworking friend.

The one thing you shouldn't worry about is your skill level. Every project in this book is well within reach of even beginning woodworkers. Nevertheless, if you've never built anything with wood before, you may want to start with a small project, such as the squirrel feeder on page 50 or the seedling trays on page 87. Your confidence—and your workmanship—will grow with every project you build.

▼ MATERIALS AND SUPPLIES
(or sometimes just Materials)

This list specifies the total amount of wood you'll need in linear feet, as well as any additional supplies such, as wood glue or caulk. To cover waste and account for squaring ends, we've allowed a slight overage in the number of feet required. Even so, it's not a bad idea to overbuy by ten to twenty percent; you can always use leftovers for your next project. Be sure to check the Cutting List before buying your lumber; you can buy 24 linear feet of 2 x 4 cedar several ways, but if the Cutting List

calls for seven-foot lengths, you should buy three eight-foot 2 x 4's rather than four six-foot 2 x 4's .

▼ HARDWARE

This list tells you the exact number and type of nails, screws, and other hardware needed to build the project. You'll buy hardware by the pound or by the box, but this list will give you a reference amount. As with lumber, it's always a good idea to have a extras on hand.

▼ ADDITIONAL TOOLS

On page 16, you saw a basic Tool Box that listed the tools you should have on hand for the projects in this book. Some projects require one or more additional tools that aren't included in the Tool Box; if that's the case, an "Additional Tools" list will accompany the project.

▼ CUTTING LIST

This is a precise guide for cutting each piece in the project. It's arranged as a five-column chart with the following headings: Code, Description, Quantity (Qty.), Material, and Dimensions. The code is the letter (A, B, C, etc.) that identifies each piece in the illustration(s); it also appears with the first mention of each piece in each step of the instructions. The description is the name by which the piece is called in the instructions, where it's always shown in bold-faced type. Quantity tells you how many of that piece you'll need to cut, and the material column tells you from what material to cut it. The material column also tells you a lot about the dimensions of the piece. For instance, if you're cutting a piece from a 2 x 4, the piece will have the thickness of a 2 x 4—which is $1\frac{1}{2}$ inches. (See the "Softwood Lumber Sizes" chart on page 10.) If you're simply cutting a length from the 2 x 4, the dimensions column will list just a length, and you'll know that the piece has the same width as the material from which it's cut. If a piece requires more than a simple crosscut, the dimension column will also give a width, and the directions will tell you when to make the rip cut. When it's included in the dimension column, the width always comes first.

Wait to cut the pieces until the instructions tell you to do so. Before cutting a piece, figure out where it will go and check it against the actual fit—not just the Cutting List; this way, you can make the minor adjustments that will result in a well-crafted project.

▼ THE INSTRUCTIONS

The step-by-step instructions in this book are written for basic tools. If you're an advanced woodworker who has a fully equipped workshop and stationary power tools, you'll probably want to adjust the procedures accordingly. Just remember to "translate" our directions for use with your tools.

Regardless of your skill level, always read the instructions all the way through before starting. Check for unfamiliar procedures or techniques; if you find any, look them up in the index and re-read about them in the Woodworking Basics chapter. If you still feel uncomfortable, ask a friend who has a lot of woodworking experience, or refer to a basic woodworking-techniques book.

▼ THE ILLUSTRATIONS

As you've probably already noticed, each project in this book is accompanied by at least one comprehensive, exploded-view illustration. These illustrations will probably help you more than any other single element in the book. They're designed to show parts of the projects that may not be obvious from the photos or the instructions. For instance, when a piece can't be seen from the "outside" of the project, in the illustration it's represented by dotted lines and labeled

with a white code letter. Pieces that *can* be seen from the "outside" are shown with solid lines and labeled with black code letters. Before you start a project, be sure to study its illustration thoroughly and refer to it often to make sure you understand where pieces will fit and how they should be oriented.

One Final Tip

Don't be discouraged if you make a few mistakes! Even the most experienced woodworker sometimes cuts a piece $\frac{1}{8}$ inch too short, or pounds a thumb instead of a nail. These errors are part of the learning process, and you should think of them that way. Stay alert, though. If you find yourself making more than a few casual blunders, take a break. Come back to your project when your mind is clear and you're able to focus. Your project will turn out better, you'll be more satisfied with the work, and you'll stand a much better chance of hitting the nail instead of your thumb!

BUTTERFLY BOX

When you're cozied up inside on a wet, chilly day, where do all the other creatures go? Into this handsome butterfly box, if they're lucky. Butterflies seek out cracks and crevices anywhere they can. Mounting this sleek construction near plants that butterflies love will ensure a safe haven for some of summer's most welcome guests.

▼ RECOMMENDED MATERIAL

Exterior-grade plywood for the thin spacers (B); cedar or pine for all other pieces

▼ RECOMMENDED FINISH

Exterior stain

▼ MATERIALS AND SUPPLIES

13 linear feet of 1 x 6 stock

1 piece of ½-inch exterior-grade plywood, 3" x 5"

Exterior wood glue

▼ HARDWARE

8   3d finishing nails

16   1¼" decking screws

2   1⅝" decking screws

▼ ADDITIONAL TOOL

Chisel or low-angle block plane

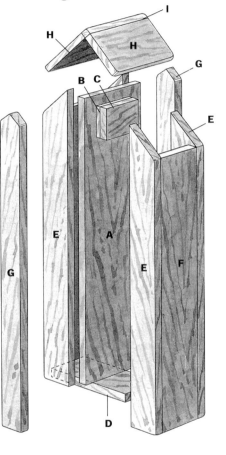

INSTRUCTIONS

1. Cut the **middle** (A), two **thin spacers** (B), and two **thick spacers** (C).

2. Glue a **thin spacer** (B) to each **thick spacer** (C), edges and ends flush, to create two spacer assemblies. Clamp each assembly together while the glue cures.

3. Remove the clamps from the spacer assemblies. Then position a spacer assembly face-to-face against the **middle** (A), centered widthwise, with its top edge 1 inch down from one end of the **middle**. (This is the **middle's** top end.) The spacer assembly's 2¼-inch ends should be parallel to the **middle's** edges. Attach the spacer assembly to the **middle** with a 1⅝-inch screw.

4. Attach the remaining spacer assembly to the other face of the **middle** (A), directly opposite the first spacer assembly.

5. Cut a 3-inch length from 1 x 6 stock. Rip the 5¼-inch-wide **floor** (D) from this piece.

6. Using the illustration as a guide, center the bottom end of the **middle** (A) across the face of the **floor** (D).

▼ CUTTING LIST

CODE	DESCRIPTION	QTY.	MATERIAL	DIMENSIONS
A	Middle	1	1 x 6 stock	21¾" long
B	Thin spacers	2	½" plywood	2¼" x 3"
C	Thick spacers	2	1 x 6 stock	2¼" x 3"
D	Floor	1	1 x 6 stock	5¼" x 3"
E	Sides	4	1 x 6 stock	2½" x 22"
F	Doors	2	1 x 6 stock	3" x 19⅝"
G	Fronts	2	1 x 6 stock	2¼" x 23"
H	Roof pieces	2	1 x 6 stock	9" long
I	Roof strip	1	1 x 6 stock	¾" x 9"

DESIGNER: **ROBIN CLARK**

The edges of the **middle** should extend beyond the edges of the **floor** by $1\frac{1}{4}$ inches on each side. Attach the pieces with a $1\frac{1}{4}$-inch screw, $\frac{1}{2}$ inch in from each edge of the **floor**, centered over the edge of the **middle**. This is the middle-floor assembly.

7. Cut two 22-inch lengths from 1 x 6 stock. From each length, rip two $2\frac{1}{2}$-inch-wide pieces to produce the four **sides** (E).

8. On one face of each **side** (E), mark and cut a 45° angle from the corner of one end to the opposite edge. This angled end will be the top end of each **side**. Sand the edges smooth and round them slightly.

9. Cut two $19\frac{5}{8}$-inch lengths from 1 x 6 stock. Rip a 3-inch-wide **door** (F) from each length. Save one of the $2\frac{1}{2}$-inch x $19\frac{5}{8}$-inch scraps for use in step 21.

10. Position a **side** (E) against a **door** (F), ends even, with the face of the **door** flush with the shorter edge of the **side**. (See the illustration.) Attach the pieces with a $1\frac{1}{4}$-inch screw through the face of the **side**, centered over the edge of the door, locating the screw $1\frac{1}{4}$ inches down from the **side's** top end.

11. Attach a **side** (E) to the **door's** (F) other edge, making sure that the **sides'** angles are parallel. The **door** should swivel easily between the **sides**, which will allow you to open and clean the butterfly house.

12. Use a low-angle block plane or a sharp wood chisel to bevel the top outside corner of the **door** (F) even with the angle on the **sides** (E).

13. Repeat steps 10–12 to make a second side-door assembly with the remaining **sides** (E) and **door** (F).

14. Position a side-door assembly against one end of the middle-floor assembly. The inside face of the **door** (F) should be against the end of the **floor** (D), and the bottom ends of the **door** and **sides** (E) should be flush with the **floor's** bottom face. Attach the assemblies with a $1\frac{1}{4}$-inch screw through each **side**, into the adjoining edge of the **floor**.

15. Drive two 3d finishing nails through the face of each **side** (E) and into the adjoining edge of the spacer assembly.

16. Repeat steps 14 and 15 at the other end of the middle-floor assembly with the remaining side-door assembly.

17. Cut a 23-inch length from 1 x 6 stock. Rip two $2\frac{1}{4}$-inch-wide **fronts** (G) from this length.

18. On each **front** (G), find the center, widthwise, and mark a line there across the length. At one end of each **front**, mark a 45° angle from the center line to each edge. Cut to these lines to form the point at the top of each **front**. Sand the edges smooth and round them slightly.

19. Glue a **front** (G) to each edge of the **middle** (A). The face of each **front** should be centered over one edge of the **middle**, and the bottom ends of the **fronts** should be flush with the bottom ends of the **sides** (E). This completes the body of the butterfly house.

20. Cut two **roof pieces** (H).

21. Cut a 9-inch length from the scrap you saved from step 9. Rip the $\frac{3}{4}$-inch-wide **roof strip** (I) from this length.

22. Center a **roof piece** (H) over the top of one side of the butterfly house body. The top edge of the **roof piece** should be flush with one angled side of the top end of the **fronts** (G), and the ends of the **roof piece** should extend beyond the outside faces of the **sides** (E) by $2\frac{1}{4}$ inches at each end. Attach the pieces with two $1\frac{1}{4}$-inch screws through the face of the **roof piece**, centered over and into the ends of both adjoining **sides**.

23. Repeat step 22 to attach the remaining **roof piece** (H) to the other side of the butterfly house box.

24. Place the **roof strip** (I) in the space between the **roof pieces** (H). Attach the **roof strip** with two $1\frac{1}{4}$-inch screws through its edge, into the adjoining **roof piece**.

25. Sand smooth and round over all the roof's exposed edges and ends. Then finish the butterfly box with the stain of your choice.

ORIENTAL PLANT PEDESTAL

Elegant, but very easy to make, this gorgeous project will showcase your favorite plant to its best advantage. Ceramic tiles give this Oriental-style pedestal a unique decorative touch that's missing from most commercial plant stands. You can easily customize your project's look simply by changing the tile color and configuration.

▼ **RECOMMENDED MATERIAL**

T-1-11 exterior siding for the sides (C) and top (G); cedar or pine for all other pieces

▼ **RECOMMENDED FINISH**

Clear water sealer for cedar or pine parts (The pieces made from exterior siding will not require a finish.)

▼ **MATERIALS AND SUPPLIES**

1 piece of $\frac{3}{8}$-inch exterior siding, 4' x 4'

16 linear feet of 2 x 2 stock

18 linear feet of 1 x 1 stock

7 linear feet of 2 x 4 stock

10 ceramic tiles, each 2" x 2"

Clear silicone caulk

▼ **HARDWARE**

32   $1\frac{1}{4}$" decking screws

8   1" decking screws

60   8d finishing nails

▼ **ADDITIONAL TOOLS**

Miter box

Jigsaw or coping saw with a fine blade

Miter square

Help from a friend

DESIGNER: **MARK STROM**

▼ CUTTING LIST

CODE	DESCRIPTION	QTY.	MATERIAL	DIMENSIONS
A	Legs	4	2 x 2 stock	28¾" long
B	Leg strips	8	1 x 1 stock	23¾" long
C	Sides	4	⅜" siding	10" x 24"
D	Top-support strips	4	1 x 1 stock	8½" long
E	Upper border pieces	4	2 x 4 stock	2" x 18"
F	Lower border pieces	4	2 x 2 stock	16" long
G	Top	1	⅜" siding	12" x 12"

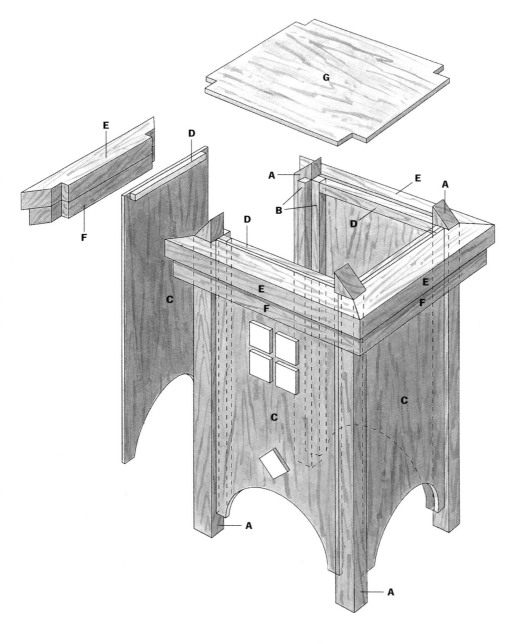

INSTRUCTIONS

1. Cut four **legs** (A). On one end of each **leg**, mark and cut a 45° angle. This is the top end of the **leg**.

2. Lay out the **legs** (A) in two pairs, with their ends even. The angles on each pair should face away from each other. You'll make a side panel from each pair in step 9.

3. Measure 3 inches up from the bottom end of each **leg** (A) and mark this point on the upper face and the inner face of each piece. These marks will show you where to attach the **leg strips** (B) in the next step.

4. Cut eight **leg strips** (B). Place a **leg strip** against each **leg** (A), with its bottom end at the 3-inch line you marked in step 3. The edge of each **leg strip** should be about ⅛ inch from the upper inside corner of each **leg**.

5. Attach each **leg strip** (B) to the adjoining **leg** (A) with five evenly spaced 1¼-inch finishing nails.

6. Cut four **sides** (C). Find the center, widthwise, of each **side** and mark this point on one end. This will be the bottom end of the **side**.

7. Use a compass to trace a 4⅛-inch-radius semicircle on the bottom end of each **side** (C), using the center mark that you made in step 6 to place the pointed end of the compass.

8. Cut out the semicircle on each **side** (C) with a jigsaw or coping saw.

9. To make two side panels, start by placing a **side** (C) between each set of **legs** (A), on top of the **leg strips** (B). The flat end of each **side** should be flush with the top ends of the **leg strips**. Screw through the **side** into the **leg strips**, using four evenly spaced 1¼-inch screws along each joint. You now have two side panels.

10. You may need a friend to help with this step and the next one. Place the side panels on edge with their inside faces toward each other and their ends even. Place one of the remaining **sides** (C) between the two side panels, on top of the upper **leg strips** (B). Make sure that its top and bottom ends are even with the top and bottom ends of the adjacent **sides**. Ask your friend to hold the panels in place.

11. Screw through the **side** (C) into the **leg strips** (B), using four evenly spaced 1¼-inch screws along each of the **side's** edges. Turn this assembly over and attach the remaining **side** the same way. You should now have a box.

12. Cut four **top-support strips** (D). Place a **top-support strip** at the top end of each **side** (C), centering it between the two **leg strips** (B). The upper edge of the **top-support strip** should be flush with the top end of the **side**. Attach each **top-support strip** to the side with three $1\frac{1}{4}$-inch finishing nails into the adjoining **side**

13. Cut four **upper border pieces** (E).

14. To cut the notches in the **upper border pieces** (E) (see the illustration), start by holding one piece, centered lengthwise, against the **legs** (A) at the top of one side. Mark the piece and the **side** (C) with a number or letter to show that this **upper border piece** will be installed against that **side**.

15. Mark the points at which the inside corners of the **legs** (A) touch the **upper border piece** (E). Square these marks across the top and inside face of the **upper border piece**.

16. Cut rectangular notches from these points to the ends of the piece to allow the **upper border piece** (E) to fit against the **side** (C). The notches will measure approximately $\frac{1}{2}$ x 4 inches, but you must measure the offset between each **leg** (A) and its adjoining **side** to avoid leaving gaps when the **upper border piece** is installed.

17. Fit the **upper border piece** (E) against the **side** (C), with its top surface $\frac{3}{8}$ inch above the top of the **side**. Mark the **upper border piece** at the outside corners of the legs. If the corners of the legs are rounded, you must visualize where the miter cut will begin.

18. Using a miter square, mark the miters on the top of the **upper border piece** (E) outward to its outside edge. Use a miter box to cut the miters.

19. To fit the remaining **upper border pieces** (E), repeat steps 14–18. Clamp the completed **upper border pieces** in place at the top of their **sides** (C) when you need them to help mark the adjoining miters.

20. Cut four **lower border pieces** (F). Use the procedures in steps 14–18 to cut notches and miters, fitting the **lower border pieces** to their positions around the sides and legs.

21. Cut the **top** (G) after checking its dimensions against the tops of the **sides** (C). The edges of the **top** will be flush with the outside faces of the **sides**.

22. To cut the notches at each corner of the **top** (G), start by measuring and marking 1 inch in and 1 inch over at each corner. This will result in a 1-inch square at each corner.

23. Before cutting the notches at the corners of the **top** (G), check them against the **legs** (A). If necessary, adjust the notches; then cut them with a handsaw or jigsaw.

24. Place the **top** (G) on the box, fitting its notches around the **legs** (A). Screw through the **top** into the **top-support strips** (D) below, using two 1-inch screws at each joint.

25. Using the illustration as a guide, fit an **upper border piece** (E) against and between two **legs** (A), with its top surface flush with the **top** (G). Secure the pieces with one 8d finishing nail through the edge of the **upper border piece** into the **leg**. Making sure that the top faces of each piece are flush, repeat with the remaining three **upper border pieces**. When all the **upper border pieces** are in place, drive a nail through the end of each one, across the miter joint, into the adjoining end of the next piece.

26. Using the same method as in step 25, attach the **lower border pieces** (F) to the **legs** (A), directly under the **upper border pieces** (E).

27. Sand the stock portions of the plant stand smooth; then finish them with a clear oil finish.

28. Using the project photo and the illustration as a guide, attach the ceramic tiles to two opposite **sides** (C) with clear silicone caulk.

BLUEBIRD HOUSE

Entice a family of bluebirds to share your garden space by installing this inviting project on a post or in a tall tree. (Placing the birdhouse in a short tree with low branches might expose its inhabitants to unwelcome feline exploration.) One side of the house pivots open on two screws for easy spring cleaning, the floor is designed to provide ventilation and drainage, and the "entry door" is sized just right for most small songbird species.

▼ **RECOMMENDED MATERIAL**

Cedar or pine

▼ **RECOMMENDED FINISH**

Green exterior paint for the narrow roof (F) and the wide roof (G), and exterior stain for all other pieces

▼ **MATERIALS**

6 linear feet of 1 x 6 stock

▼ **HARDWARE**

14 1¼" decking screws
1 1" hook-and-eye set

▼ **CUTTING LIST**

CODE	DESCRIPTION	QTY.	MATERIAL	DIMENSIONS
A	Front	1	1 x 6 stock	11⅜" long
B	Entry	1	1 x 6 stock	3½" x 3½"
C	Sides	2	1 x 6 stock	4" x 8⁵⁄₁₆"
D	Floor	1	1 x 6 stock	4" x 4"
E	Back	1	1 x 6 stock	13½" long
F	Narrow roof	1	1 x 6 stock	4½" x 6½"
G	Wide roof	1	1 x 6 stock	6½" long

INSTRUCTIONS

1. Cut the **front** (A). Find its center, widthwise, and mark a line there along its length.

2. From one end of the **front** (A), mark a 45° angle from the center line to each edge. Cut to these lines to form the point at the top of the **front**. Sand the uncut edges smooth and round them slightly.

3. Cut a 3½-inch length from 1 x 6 stock. Rip the 3½-inch-square **entry** (B) from this length.

4. Place the **entry** (B) against the **front** (A) at the **front's** top end, with the **entry's** edges flush with the **front's** edges as shown in the illustration. Clamp the pieces in place. Screw through the **front** into the **entry**, with one 1¼-inch screw at each of the **entry's** corners.

5. To make the round door, use a drill with a 1½-inch spade bit to bore a centered hole through the **entry** (B). Bore until the tip of the bit begins to emerge from the back face of the **front** (A). Finish the hole by boring from the back face of the **front**.

6. Cut two 8⁵⁄₁₆-inch lengths from 1 x 6 stock. Rip the two 4-inch-wide **sides** (C) from these lengths.

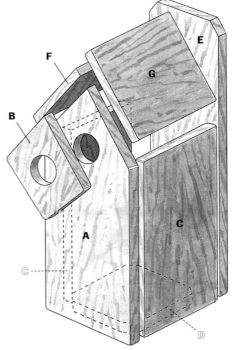

7. Place the edge of one **side** (C) against the back face of the **front** (A), with the **side's** face flush with the **front's** edge and their bottom ends even. Clamp the pieces in place. Measuring up $7\frac{3}{4}$-inches from **front's** bottom end, screw through the **front** into the edge of the **side**, with a $1\frac{1}{4}$-inch screw.

8. Repeat step 7 to attach the second **side** (C) to the **front's** (A) other edge.

9. Cut a 4-inch length from 1 x 6 stock. Rip the 4-inch-square **floor** (D) from this length.

10. To cut the angles on the corners of the **floor** (D), start by marking points on all four sides of the face, $\frac{1}{2}$ inch in from each corner. Mark a line between the points, across each corner, and cut to these lines.

11. Position the **floor** (D) inside the front-side assembly, with its bottom face about $\frac{3}{4}$ inch up from the bottom ends of the **front** (A) and **sides** (C). Clamp the pieces in place.

12. Screw through the **front** (A), into the adjacent edge of the **floor** (D), with one $1\frac{1}{4}$-inch screw. Then screw through one **side** (C) into the adjacent edge of the **floor**, with one centered $1\frac{1}{4}$-inch screw.

13. Cut the **back** (E) and position it against the rear edges of the **sides** (C), edges flush with the **sides'** faces, and bottom ends even. Clamp the pieces in place.

14. Measuring $7\frac{3}{4}$ inches up from the **back's** (E) bottom end, screw through the **back** into the adjacent edges of the **sides** (C), using one $1\frac{1}{4}$-inch screw at each joint.

15. Cut a $6\frac{1}{2}$-inch length from 1 x 6 stock. Rip the $4\frac{1}{2}$-inch-wide **narrow roof** (F) from this length.

16. Place the **narrow roof** (F) over one side of the top of the birdhouse, top edge flush with one angled side of the **entry** (B), and one end against the **back's** (E) front face. Clamp the pieces in place. Screw through the **narrow roof** into the edge of the **front** (A), with one $1\frac{1}{4}$-inch screw.

17. Cut the **wide roof** (G) and place it over the other half of the birdhouse. The top edge of the **wide roof** should be flush with the face of the **narrow roof** (F), and their ends should be even. Clamp the pieces in place. Screw through the **wide roof** into the edge of the **narrow roof**, with one $1\frac{1}{4}$-inch screw. Then screw through the **wide roof** into the angled end of the **front** (A), with one $1\frac{1}{4}$-inch screw.

18. Screw through the **back** (E) into the adjacent ends of the **narrow roof** (F) and the **wide roof** (G), using one $1\frac{1}{4}$-inch screw at each joint.

19. Sand the project smooth and round all the exposed edges slightly before finishing with a stain or sealer.

20. To achieve a weathered look on the painted roof, sand the roof well, paint it, and let the paint dry completely; then sand the roof lightly a second time.

21. To "lock" the **side** (C) that pivots open, attach the hook-and-eye set, screwing one piece into the face of the pivoting **side**, and the other piece into the adjoining edge of the **back** (E), both about 1 inch up from the birdhouse's bottom end.

ELEGANT PLANTER

A beautiful plant deserves an equally lovely planter. Even your most prized flowers will feel right at home in this stunning, yet simple-to-build project. The project shown in the photo is an excellent example of how to turn the flaws in a lower grade of lumber into attractive features. Far from detracting from this project's beauty, the numerous knots in the wood that the designer selected actually add to the planter's elegant appearance.

▼ RECOMMENDED MATERIAL

Exterior-grade plywood for the plant rest (E); cedar or pine for all other pieces

▼ RECOMMENDED FINISH

Clear oil wood finish

▼ MATERIALS AND SUPPLIES

40 linear feet of 2 x 4 stock

3½ linear feet of 1 x 2 stock

5½ linear feet of 1 x 6 stock

1 piece of ½-inch exterior plywood, 10⅜" x 11"

▼ HARDWARE

32 6d finishing nails

62 10d finishing nails

14 1½" decking screws

▼ ADDITIONAL TOOLS

Miter box

Jigsaw or coping saw with a fine blade

▼ CUTTING LIST

CODE	DESCRIPTION	QTY.	MATERIAL	DIMENSIONS
A	Vertical side pieces	14	2 x 4 stock	21" long
B	Long foot pieces	2	2 x 4 stock	11" long
C	Short foot pieces	2	2 x 4 stock	7½" long
D	Side braces	4	1 x 2 stock	9" long
E	Plant rest	1	½" plywood	10⅜" x 11"
F	Short arch pieces	2	1 x 6 stock	13½" long
G	Long arch pieces	2	1 x 6 stock	15½" long
H	Short top pieces	2	2 x 4 stock	17½" long
I	Long top pieces	2	2 x 4 stock	18" long

INSTRUCTIONS

1. Cut fourteen **vertical side pieces** (A).

2. On a flat surface, clamp together four of the **vertical side pieces** (A), edge to edge, with their ends even.

3. From what will be the bottom end of the **vertical side pieces** (A), measure 1½ inch from one end and square a line across all four boards at this point.

4. At the bottom end of the two outermost **vertical side pieces** (A), measure in 1½ inches from the outside edge of each piece and mark this point across the line that you made in step 3. These marks will show you where to attach the **long foot piece** (B).

5. Cut two **long foot pieces** (B).

6. Place one **long foot piece** (B) across the four-board side panel, with its top edge below the line on the **vertical side pieces** (A) from step 3 and its ends between the lines from step 4. The bottom edge of the **long foot piece** will overlap the bottom ends of the **vertical side pieces** by 2 inches.

7. Attach the **long foot piece** (B) with two 10d finishing nails into each **vertical side piece** (A). This will be the inside face of the side panel.

DESIGNER: **MARK STROM**

8. Repeat steps 2–4 and 6–7 to make a second four-board side panel.

9. On a flat surface, clamp together three **vertical side pieces** (A), edge to edge, with their ends even.

10. From what will be the bottom end of the **vertical side pieces** (A), measure 1½ inches from one end of the boards and square a line across all three at this point.

11. At the bottom end of the two outer **vertical side pieces** (A), measure in 1½ inches from the outside edge of each piece and mark this point across the line that you made in step 10. These marks will show you where to attach the **short foot piece** (C).

12. Cut two **short foot pieces** (C).

13. Place one **short foot piece** (C) across the three **vertical side pieces** (A), with its top edge below the line from step 10 and its ends between the lines from step 11. The bottom edge of the **short foot piece** will overlap the bottom ends of the **vertical side pieces** by 2 inches.

14. Attach the **short foot piece** (B) with two 10d finishing nails into each **vertical side piece** (A).

15. Repeat steps 9–11 and 13–14 to make the second three-board side panel.

16. On the inside face of each side panel, measure 12 inches up from the bottom edges of the **foot pieces** (B and C) and mark a line across all the boards at this point.

17. Cut four **side braces** (D).

18. On each side panel, place a **side brace** (D) facedown above the line that you marked in step 16, centering the **side brace** across the boards. Screw through each **side brace** into the adjacent **vertical side piece** (A), using one 1½-inch screw at each **vertical side piece**.

19. Using the illustration as a guide, form a box from the side panels by placing the three-board panels between the four-board panels. Be sure to line up all their bottom and top ends. Clamp the panels together; then nail them in place with five evenly spaced 10d finishing nails through each joint.

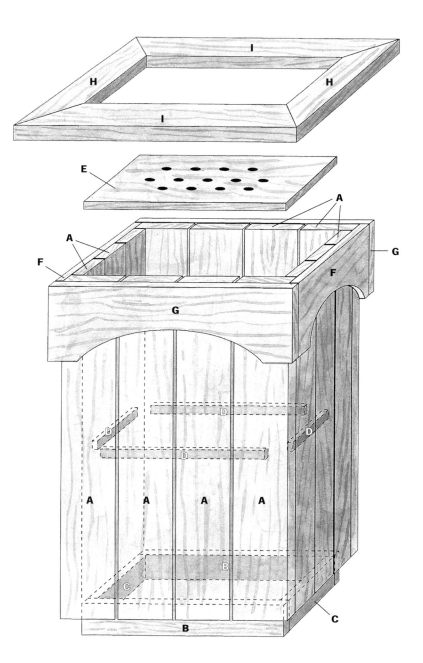

20. Bore ten to fifteen ⅜-inch holes through the **plant rest** (E) to provide drainage for the planter's future inhabitant.

21. Place the **plant rest** (E) inside the box, so that it rests on top of the **side braces** (D).

22. Cut two **short arch pieces** (F).

23. To mark the arches on the **short arch pieces** (F), start by laying the two pieces on a flat surface, edge to edge and ends even.

24. Find the center of both **short arch pieces** (F) lengthwise and square this point across the width of the boards.

25. Set your compass to a 7½-inch radius and place the point of the compass on the center line of the outside edge of one **short arch piece** (F). Scribe an arc on the inside edge of the other **short arch piece**. Then place the compass point at the center of the outside edge of the **short arch piece** that you just marked and scribe an arc on the inside edge of the other **short arch piece**. Use a jigsaw or a coping saw to cut the arcs.

26. Cut two **long arch pieces** (G), and repeat steps 24–25 to mark and cut the arcs on them.

27. Place a **short arch piece** (F) across the top of one three-board side panel, straight edge flush with the top ends of the **vertical side pieces** (A).

28. Drive a 6d finishing nail through the **short arch piece** (F) into the edges of the **vertical side pieces** (A) on the adjoining four-board side panels. Then drive two 6d finishing nails through the **short arch piece** into the face of each adjacent **vertical side piece** in the three-board side panel.

29. Repeat steps 27–28 on the opposite three-board side panel with the remaining **short arch piece** (F).

30. Place a **long arch piece** (G) across the top of one four-board side panel, straight edge flush with the top ends of the **vertical side pieces** (A).

31. Drive a 6d finishing nail through the **long arch piece** (G) into the edge of each of the two adjoining **short arch pieces** (F). Then drive two 6d finishing nails through the **long arch piece** into the face of each of the adjacent **vertical side pieces** in the four-board side panel.

32. Repeat steps 30–31 on the opposite four-board side with the remaining **long arch piece** (G).

33. Cut two **short top pieces** (H).

34. On each **short top piece** (H), mark a 45° angle across one face at each end. Check your marks against piece H in the illustration to make sure you've marked the angles correctly. Cut the angles, using a miter box to assure accuracy.

35. Cut two **long top pieces** (I).

36. On each **long top piece** (I), mark a 45° angle across the face at each end. Check your marks against piece I in the illustration to make sure you've marked the angles correctly. Cut the angles, using a miter box to assure accuracy.

37. Arrange the **short top pieces** (H) and the **long top pieces** (I) into a rectangle, with the ends of the pieces forming miter joints, as shown in the illustration. Clamp the pieces in place.

38. Fasten the pieces of the rectangle formed by the **short** and **long top pieces** (H and I) with a 6d finishing nail through both edges across each joint.

39. Place the rectangle from step 38 on top of the box, with the inside edges of the **short** and **long top pieces** (H and I) flush with the inside faces of the **vertical side pieces** (A).

40. Fasten the rectangle in place with 10d nails through the faces of the **short** and **long top pieces** (H and I), driving a nail into the end of each adjacent **vertical side piece** (A).

41. Sand the planter and finish the project with a waterproof finish.

SQUIRREL FEEDER

Invite your favorite furry friend to pull up a seat at its very own garden café. This clever project will keep resident squirrels happily occupied—and safely away from the local avian diners!

▼RECOMMENDED MATERIAL

Cedar or pine

▼RECOMMENDED FINISH

Clear water sealer

▼MATERIALS AND SUPPLIES

4 linear feet of 1 x 4 stock

1 dried corncob

▼HARDWARE

2   $1\frac{1}{4}$" decking screws

6   $1\frac{5}{8}$" decking screws

3   $2\frac{1}{2}$" decking screws

▼CUTTING LIST

CODE	DESCRIPTION	QTY.	MATERIAL	DIMENSIONS
A	Back	1	1 x 4 stock	14" long
B	Brace	1	1 x 4 stock	$3\frac{1}{2}$" square
C	Base	1	1 x 4 stock	8" long
D	Cob holder	1	1 x 4 stock	$3\frac{1}{2}$" square
E	Seat support	1	1 x 4 stock	$1\frac{1}{4}$" long
F	Seat	1	1 x 4 stock	$3\frac{1}{2}$" square

INSTRUCTIONS

1. Cut all the pieces (A–F).

2. To cut the angles at each corner on the **back** (A), start by measuring $\frac{3}{4}$ inch from the corner on both sides of each corner. Mark a line between the points at each corner and cut to this line. Sand the cut edges smooth.

3. Refer to piece B in the illustration. To cut the angle on the **brace** (B), use the same technique described in step 2, marking points $2\frac{1}{2}$ inches from the corner on both sides of one corner. Sand the cut edge smooth.

4. Using the illustration as a guide, center one end of the **brace** (B) over one face of the **base** (C), with the straight edge of the **brace** flush with one end of the **base**. Screw through the **base** into the end of the **brace**, using one $1\frac{5}{8}$-inch screw.

5. Drive a $2\frac{1}{2}$-inch screw through the center of the **cob holder** (D). This screw will hold the corncob.

6. Using the illustration as a guide, position the **cob holder** (D), screw side up, against the **base** (C) at the face and end opposite the **brace** (B). The end of the **cob holder** should be flush with the end of the **base**, and the **cob holder**'s edges should be flush with the **base**'s edges. Screw through the **base** (C) into the **cob holder**, using two $1\frac{1}{4}$-inch screws.

7. Position the base assembly against the **back** (A), with the bottom end of the **brace** (B) about $1\frac{1}{2}$ inches from the bottom end of the **back**. The edges of the **base** (C) should be flush with the **back**'s edges. Screw through the **back** into the end of the **base**, using two $1\frac{5}{8}$-inch screws. Then screw through the **back** into the edge of the **brace**, using one $1\frac{5}{8}$-inch screw.

8. Referring to the illustration, place the **seat support** (E) edge-down on the **base** (C), with its inside edge about $2\frac{3}{4}$ inches in from the outside face of the **back** (A). The **seat support**'s ends should be flush with the **base**'s edges.

9. Place the **seat** (F) on top of the **seat support** (E), butting the **seat**'s end against the **back**'s (A) face. Clamp the pieces in place. Screw through the bottom face of the **base** (C) through the edge of the **seat support** and into the face of the **seat**, using two $2\frac{1}{2}$-inch screws.

10. Sand all of the squirrel feeder's edges smooth and finish as desired.

11. Stick a cob of dried corn on the screw in the **cob holder** (D), find a tree that's popular with the local squirrel population, and mount the project by nailing it to the tree.

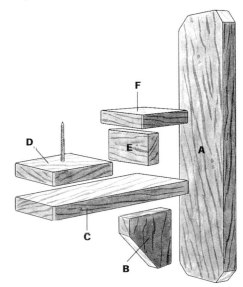

DESIGNER: **ROBIN CLARK**

TRELLIS

This unique trellis can hide an unsightly wall, enhance an empty corner of your lawn, or create shade where there once was none. The unusual design is so easy to build that you'll probably want to make more than one!

▼ CUTTING LIST

CODE	DESCRIPTION	QTY.	MATERIAL	DIMENSIONS
A	Frame pieces	2	2 x 2 PT stock	96" long
B	Crosspieces	8	1 x 2 PT stock	48" long
C	Spacers	2	1 x 2 PT stock	48" long
D	Verticals	6	1 x 2 PT stock	96" long
E	Curved lattices	4	1 x 2 PT stock	48" long
F	Short spacers	4	1 x 2 PT stock	3" long
G	30" lattice	5	1 x 2 PT stock	30" long
H	18" lattice	16	1 x 2 PT stock	18" long
I	6" lattice	16	1 x 2 PT stock	6" long
J	10¾" lattice	2	1 x 2 PT stock	10¾" long
K	8" lattice	2	1 x 2 PT stock	8" long
L	Stakes	2	2 x 2 PT stock	72" long

▼ RECOMMENDED MATERIAL
Pressure-treated pine or spruce

▼ RECOMMENDED FINISH
Clear water sealer or exterior paint

▼ MATERIALS AND SUPPLIES
28 linear feet of 2 x 2 PT stock (Purchase this in two 2 x 2 x 8' pieces and two 2 x 2 x 6' pieces.)

168 linear feet of 1 x 2 PT stock (Purchase this in twenty-one 1 x 2 x 8' pieces.)

1 piece of cardboard, 24" x 24"

1 sheet of plywood (optional), 4' x 8'

▼ HARDWARE
486 3d finishing nails

32 6d finishing nails

12 3" decking screws

▼ ADDITIONAL TOOL
Jigsaw or coping saw with a fine blade

INSTRUCTIONS

1. Because this project consists of so many pieces, it's an exception to the "don't cut until you have to" rule. Start by cutting all the pieces from the 2 x 2 and 1 x 2 PT stock, cutting the longest pieces from the straightest stock. Apply the finish of your choice; then label each piece.

2. On each **frame piece** (A), measure up from the bottom and mark two lines, one at 17¼ inches and one at 44¼ inches. Measuring down from the top, mark each **frame piece** at 9 inches

and at 26¼ inches. On the **crosspieces** (B), measure and mark 6 inches in from each end.

3. Position the **frame pieces** (A) parallel to each other. Place four **crosspieces** (B) across them, two with their lower edges at the 17¼-inch and 4¼-inch marks, and two with their upper edges at the 9-inch and 26¼-inch marks. Align the 6-inch marks on each **crosspiece** with the outer edge of each **frame piece**. Then fasten the **crosspieces** in place with three 3d finishing nails at each joint (All perpendicular pieces in this project are fastened in the same manner.)

4. Set one **spacer** (C), which won't be a part of the finished trellis, below the **crosspiece** (B) at the 9-inch mark, edge to edge, with its wide face down. Place another **spacer** below the **crosspiece** at the 26¼-inch mark. Then place a **crosspiece** below each **spacer**, edge to edge, leaving a 6-inch overlap at each end again. Fasten the two **crosspieces** to the **frame pieces** (A) and remove the **spacers**.

5. Set one **spacer** (C) above the **crosspiece** (B) at the 17¼-inch mark and another above the **crosspiece** at the 44¼-inch mark. Then place a

cross-piece above each **spacer**, fasten the **crosspieces** as before, and remove the **spacers**.

6. Turn the assembly over so the **frame pieces** (A) face up.

7. Measure and mark each attached **crosspiece** (B) 3 inches out from the outer edge of each **frame piece** (A).

8. Position a **vertical** (D) on the assembly, with its inner edge at one set of the 3-inch marks on the **crosspieces** (B). Position a second **vertical** on the other side of the assembly, aligning it with the 3-inch marks on the **cross-pieces** on that side. Adjust both **verticals** so their ends are aligned with the ends of the **frame pieces** (A). Then nail both **verticals** in place.

9. Place a **spacer** (C), wide face down, against the inner edge of each **frame piece** (A). Then place a **vertical** (D) with its outer edge against each **spacer's** inner edge. Adjust the verticals so their top ends are 1 inch taller than the ends of the **frame pieces**. (Their top ends will be 10 inches above the top-most **crosspiece** (B).) Nail both **verticals** in place, and remove the **spacers**.

10. Measuring in from the inner edge of each **vertical** (D) that you attached in step 9, mark each **cross-piece** (B) at 10 inches.

11. Position the two remaining **verticals** (D) with their outer edges at the 10-inch marks on the **crosspieces** (B), which will leave about 4 inches between these center **verticals**. Position them so

DESIGNER: **MARK STROM**

that their top ends are 12 inches above the topmost **crosspiece**. Nail these **verticals** in place.

12. Turn the assembly over again, so the **crosspieces** (B) are facing up.

13. Place the **short spacers** (F) on edge on the two middle **verticals** (D), with one end of each against the top **crosspiece** (B). Lay a **curved lattice** (E) on edge across the **verticals** (D), against the **short spacers**. The ends of the **curved lattice** should line up with the ends of the **crosspieces**.

14. Place a scrap of 1 x 2 under the **verticals** (D) to support them while drilling and nailing. Bore a $3/32$-inch pilot hole through the edge of the **curved lattice** (E) toward the center of each of the two middle **verticals**. Drive a 6d finish nail through each of these holes into the middle **verticals**. Use a nail set to sink the nails deeper.

15. Place a **spacer** (C) across each outside **vertical** (D) to form a $1^{1}/_{2}$-inch space above the ends of the uppermost **crosspiece** (B). Clamp one end of the **curved lattice** (E) where it is, to the outside **vertical**. Bend the other end of the **curved lattice** until it touches the **spacer**. Clamp the end of the **curved lattice** to the **spacer** and to the end of the **crosspiece**.

16. Unclamp, bend, and clamp the first end of the **curved lattice** (E) to the other **spacer** (C) and to the end of the **crosspiece** (B).

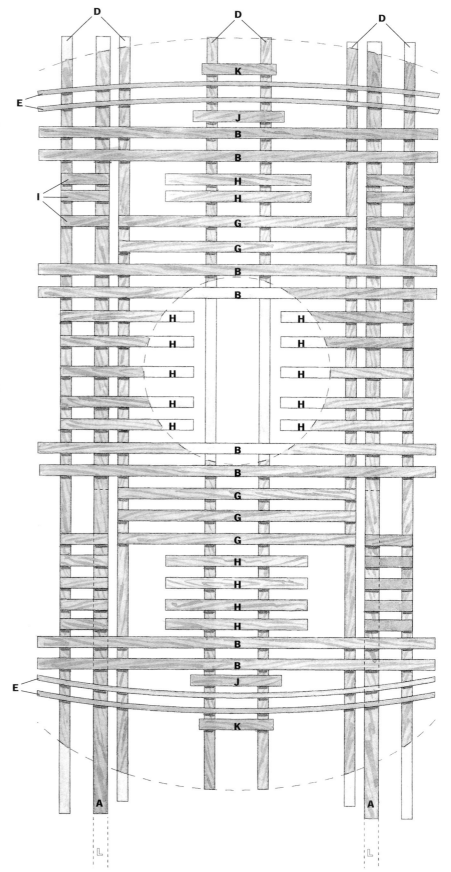

17. Bore two $3/32$-inch pilot holes at opposing angles through the edge of the **curved lattice** (E) and barely into each of the **frame pieces** (A) and **verticals** (D), including the two middle **verticals**. Drive 6d finishing nails into the holes and set them well. Remove the clamps and **spacers**.

18. Use a **spacer** (C) to position another **curved lattice** (E) $1^1/2$ inches above the first one and clamp it in place. Use two 6d finishing nails driven through pilot holes at opposing angles to fasten the **curved lattice** to each **frame piece** (A) and **vertical** (D).

19. Repeat steps 13–18 to attach the other two **curved lattices** (E) below the bottom **crosspiece** (B).

20. Using a **spacer** (C), and referring to the illustration, attach the five **30-inch lattices** (G) to the center and inner **verticals** (D). Be sure the ends of these **lattices** are even, and that each **lattice** is centered across the **verticals**.

21. Take a good look at the illustration. There are four **18-inch lattices** (H) centered across the middle **verticals** (D) at the bottom of the trellis. Using a **spacer** (C) and working downward, nail the upper three of these **lattices** in place. Position the fourth and lowest of these **18-inch lattices** by centering it in the space between the third **18-inch lattice** and the **crosspiece** (B) beneath it.

22. To attach the two **18-inch lattices** (H) at the top of the trellis, first use a **spacer** (C) to position one above the uppermost **30-inch lattice** (G). After nailing it in place, turn the spacer on edge and place one face against the **lattice** you just fastened. Then position the second **30-inch lattice** above the **spacer**, and nail it in place.

23. As you can see in the illustration, in the center of the trellis there are ten **18-inch lattices** (H) attached to the outermost and middle **verticals** (D) and to the **frame pieces** (A). Using a **spacer** (C) and working downward, first fasten the top two **18-inch lattices** on each side and the bottom two **18-inch lattices** on each side, aligning one end of each with the outside edge of an outer **vertical**. Center each of the two remaining **18-inch lattices** in the space that remains and nail them in place.

24. To attach all the **6-inch lattices** (I) to the outer **verticals** (D) and **frame pieces** (A), as shown in the illustration, just align each one with the **lattice** to its left or right.

25. At the top and bottom of the trellis, below the **curved lattices** (E) at the top, and above the **curved lattices** at the bottom, center a **$10^3/4$-inch lattice** (J) and nail it in place.

26. Using a **short spacer** (F) placed on its edge, center and fasten an **8-inch lattice** (K) across the innermost **verticals** (D), above the **curved lattices** (E) at the top of the trellis. Repeat to attach another **8-inch lattice** below the **curved lattices** at the bottom. (Both these **lattices** will overlap the innermost **verticals**).

27. Draw a 22-inch-diameter circle on the piece of cardboard and cut it out. Using the illustration as a guide, place the cardboard circle in the middle of the trellis and trace around it. Then cut out the circle with a jigsaw or a coping saw.

28. At the top of the trellis, use a jigsaw or a coping saw to trim off the ends of the four outermost **verticals** (D) and the **frame pieces** (A) to form a curved pattern. Don't trim the two **verticals** in the center of the trellis. (The dotted lines on the illustration show where to cut).

29. At the bottom of the trellis, use the jigsaw to trim the ends of all six **verticals** (D) as shown in the illustration, but don't trim the **frame pieces** (A).

30. Place a **stake** (L) face-to-face against the back face of each **frame piece** (A), with 24 inches of the **stake** extending beyond the bottom end of the **frame piece**. Screw through each **stake** into the adjoining **frame piece**, using six evenly spaced 3-inch screws at each joint.

31. To install the trellis, dig two 24-inch-deep holes, spaced to accommodate the **stakes** (K). Place the bottom ends of the **stakes** in the holes; then tightly pack the holes with dirt.

32. Even pressure-treated lumber will eventually succumb to rot, particularly if it's in direct contact with moist earth. When the buried portion of the **stakes** (K) begin to rot, simply dig up the trellis, unscrew the old **stakes**, and replace them with new ones.

ARBOR-BENCH COMBINATION

Don't let this project's size intimidate you! Constructed in six panels (the bench seat, two sides, the roof, the back, and the bench-seat back), and made entirely from standard dimension lumber assembled with simple joints, it really is a project that you can build in a weekend or two. Just remember to grab a friend to help with the final assembly!

▼ RECOMMENDED MATERIAL
Pressure-treated pine or spruce

▼ RECOMMENDED FINISH
Clear water sealer

▼ MATERIALS
12 linear feet of 2 x 6 stock
60 linear feet of 2 x 4 stock
26 linear feet of $5/4$ x 6 decking
30 linear feet of 2 x 2 stock
190 linear feet of 1 x 2 stock

▼ HARDWARE
34   3" decking screws
50    $2\frac{1}{2}$" decking screws
30   2" decking screws
372 3d finishing nails

▼ ADDITIONAL TOOLS
Large, flat work surface
Sheet of plywood
Help from at least one friend

▼ CUTTING LIST

CODE	DESCRIPTION	QTY.	MATERIAL	DIMENSION
BENCH SEAT				
A	Long seat sides	2	2 x 4 stock	45" long
B	Short seat sides	2	2 x 4 stock	23" long
C	Seat brace	1	2 x 4 stock	$14\frac{1}{2}$" long
D	Seat slats	3	$5/4$ x 6 stock	48" long
SIDE PANELS				
E	Side verticals	4	2 x 4 stock	96" long
F	Side braces	4	2 x 2 stock	23" long
G	Long side-lattice pieces	8	1 x 2 stock	84" long
H	Short side-lattice pieces	24	1 x 2 stock	23" long
ROOF				
I	Long roof horizontals	2	2 x 6 stock	72" long
J	Roof braces	2	2 x 2 stock	26" long
K	Long roof-lattice pieces	4	1 x 2 stock	60" long
L	Short roof-lattice pieces	10	1 x 2 stock	26" long
M	Short roof horizontals	2	2 x 4 stock	60" long
BACK PANEL				
N	Outside back verticals	2	1 x 2 stock	$86\frac{1}{2}$" long
O	Back horizontal	1	2 x 2 stock	42" long
P	Inside back verticals	2	2 x 2 stock	$76\frac{1}{2}$" long
Q	Back lattice pieces	14	1 x 2 stock	12" long
SEAT BACK				
R	Seat-back end frames	2	2 x 4 stock	17" long
S	Seat-back slats	3	$5\frac{1}{2}$ x $5/4$ decking	48" long

DESIGNER: **MARK STROM**

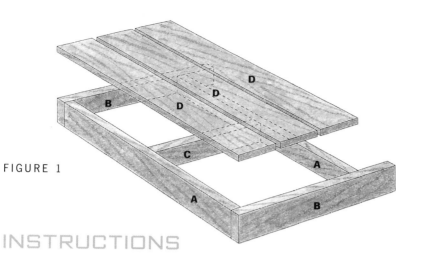

FIGURE 1

INSTRUCTIONS

BENCH SEAT
(refer to Figure 1)

1. Cut two **long seat sides** (A) and two **short seat sides** (B).

2. On a flat work surface, lay out the **short seat sides** (B) edge to edge, with their ends even. From one end, measure in 16 inches and square a line across the face of both boards at this point. The end from which you measured will be the front end of the **short seat sides** and of the assembled bench seat.

3. Turn the **short seat sides** (B) on edge, with their marked faces turned in toward each other. Position one of the **long seat sides** (A) on edge between the front ends of the **short seat sides**. The **long seat side's** ends should be butted up against the inside faces of the **short seat sides**, and its outside face should be flush with the **short seat sides'** front ends. Position the other **long seat side** on edge between the **short seat sides**, with its front face at the 16-inch lines from step 2.

4. Screw through the faces of the **short seat sides** (B) into the adjoining ends of the **long seat sides** (A), using two 3-inch screws at each joint.

5. On both **long seat sides** (A), measure in 21¾ inches from each end and strike a line across the edge of each board at this point. There should be a 1½-inch space between the two lines on each board.

6. Cut the **seat brace** (C), checking its actual length against the distance between the **long seat sides** (A) before cutting.

7. Place the **seat brace** (C) on edge between the **long seat sides** (A), faces between the lines from step 5. Screw through the outside face of each **long seat side** into the adjoining end of the **seat brace**, using two 3-inch screws at each joint. This completes the seat frame.

8. Cut three **seat slats** (D).

9. Place a **seat slat** (D) on top of the seat frame, with its outside edge flush with the face of the front **long seat side** (A), and its ends flush with the faces of the **short seat sides** (B). Screw through the **seat slat** into the adjoining edges of

the **short seat sides** and into the edge of the **seat brace** (C), using two 2-inch screws at each joint.

10. Attach a second **seat slat** (D) to the rectangular frame, ½ inch over from the first **seat slat**. Attach the last **seat slat** ½ inch over from the second **seat slat**.

SIDE PANELS
(refer to Figure 2)

11. Cut four **side verticals** (E). On a large, flat work surface, lay out the **side verticals**, edge to edge and ends even. From one end of all the **side verticals**, measure in 8½ inches and square a line across the boards at this point. The ends from which you measured will be the bottom ends of the **side verticals**. Measure in 13 inches from the top end of the **side verticals** and square a line across the boards at this point.

12. Place two of the **side verticals** (E) on edge, with their ends even and their marked faces toward each other. From the top edges of both **side verticals**, measure down 1¼ inches and 2¾ inches, and mark these points across the lines from step 11.

13. Cut two **side braces** (F). Place one **side brace** between the **side verticals** (E), bottom edge at the 8½-inch line and faces between the 1¼-inch and 2¾-inch marks. Place the other **side brace** with its top edge at the 13-inch line and its faces between the 1¼-inch and 2¾-inch marks. Use a ¾"-thick scrap under the **side braces** to keep them in position. Clamp the pieces in place.

14. Attach the **side braces** (F) by screwing through each **side vertical** (E) into the adjoining ends of the **side braces**, using one 3-inch screw at each joint.

15. On both **side braces** (F), measure in 3 inches and 8 inches from each end and square lines across the pieces at these points.

16. Cut four **long side-lattice pieces** (G). Place a **long side-lattice piece** across the **side braces** (F), inside each of the lines that you marked in step 15. The bottom ends of the **long side-lattice pieces** should be flush with the bottom edge of the bottom **side brace**, and the top ends should extend beyond the top edge of the top **side brace** by 9½ inches.

17. Use a square to check that the **long side-lattice pieces** (G) are perpendicular to the **side braces** (F), and straighten them if necessary. Then nail the **long side-lattice pieces** to the **side braces** with three 3d finishing nails through each joint. Use a scrap to back up the joint while nailing.

18. Measure 17 inches up from the bottom end of the **side verticals** (E) and square a line across the **side verticals** and the **long side-lattice pieces** (G) at this point. Measure 6½ inches up from the first line and square another line across each board. Continue to mark lines at 6½-inch intervals until you've marked twelve lines.

19. Cut twelve **short side-lattice pieces** (H). At each line from step 18, place a **short side-lattice piece** across

the **long side-lattice pieces** (G), bottom edge at the line. The ends of the **short side-lattice pieces** should touch or almost touch the inside faces of the **side verticals** (E).

20. Check that the **short side-lattice pieces** (H) are perpendicular to the **long side-lattice pieces** (G) before nailing them in place with three 3d finishing nails through each joint. (Place a support under the pieces to make hammering the nails easier.) This completes one side panel.

21. Repeat steps 12–20 to make the second side panel.

ROOF
(refer to Figure 3)

22. Cut two **long roof horizontals** (I). Refer to piece I in Figure 3 on the following page. To cut the angles on the bottom corners of the **long roof horizontals**, measure along the ends and along the bottom edges and mark points 4 inches from the corners. Draw a line between the pairs of points and cut off the triangular pieces.

23. At the top edge (the long edge) of each **long roof horizontal** (I), measure in 14¼ inches from both ends and square a line across one face of each board at this point.

24. Measure down 1¼ inches and 2¾ inches from the top edge of each **long roof horizontal** (I) and mark these points on the lines that you made in step 23.

25. Cut two **roof braces** (J). Position one **roof brace** between the **long roof**

horizontals (I), with its outer edge at one of the 14¼-inch lines, and its faces between the 1¼-inch and 2¾-inch marks. Position the remaining **roof brace** with its outer edge at the other 14¼-inch line, and its faces between the 1¼-inch and 2¾-inch lines. Use bar or pipe clamps to hold the pieces in place.

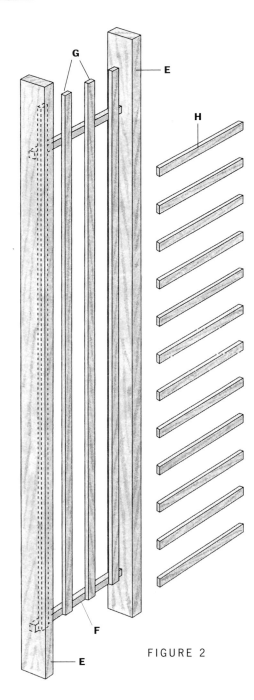

FIGURE 2

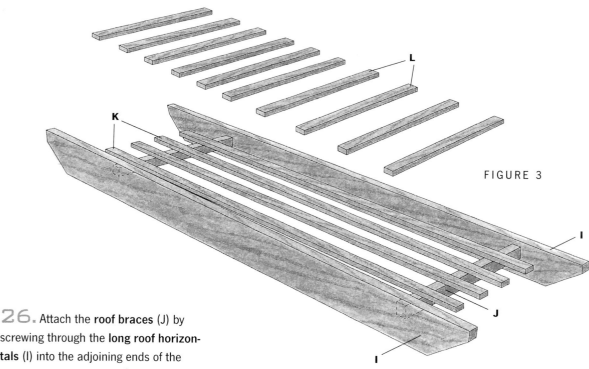

FIGURE 3

26. Attach the **roof braces** (J) by screwing through the **long roof horizontals** (I) into the adjoining ends of the **roof braces**, using one $2\frac{1}{2}$-inch screw at each joint.

27. From both ends of each **roof brace** (J) measure in $4\frac{1}{2}$ inches and $9\frac{1}{2}$ inches and mark lines across the top faces of the boards at these points.

28. Cut four **long roof-lattice pieces** (K). At each set of lines from step 27, place a **long roof-lattice piece** facedown across the **roof braces** (J), outer edge at the lines. Both ends of each **long roof-lattice piece** should extend $8\frac{1}{4}$ inches beyond the horizontal braces.

29. Check that each **long roof-lattice piece** (K) is perpendicular to the **roof braces** (J) before attaching it with three 3d finishing nails through each joint. (You will need to place a scrap of wood under the pieces to make hammering the nails easier.)

30. Cut ten **short roof-lattice pieces** (L).

31. Place one **short roof-lattice piece** (L) faceup across each end of the **long roof-lattice pieces** (K), with its outside edge even with the ends of the **long roof-lattice pieces**. Nail the two **short roof-lattice pieces** in place with three 3d finishing nails at each joint. (Use a scrap of 2 x 4 to back up the joints while you nail.)

32. Evenly arrange the eight remaining **short roof-lattice pieces** (L) faceup across the **long roof-lattice pieces** (K), leaving 5-inch spaces between all the **short roof-lattice pieces**. Make sure they are all square to the **long roof horizontals** (I), then mark their positions. Nail them in place as before.

33. Cut two **short roof horizontals** (M). Mark and cut the angles on their ends using the method described in step 22, but measuring and marking $2\frac{1}{2}$ inches (rather than 4 inches) from the bottom corners. These **short roof horizontals** are part of the roof, but you won't put them in place until step 55, so set them aside until then.

BACK PANEL
(refer to Figure 4)

34. Cut two **outside back verticals** (N). Lay them out edge to edge, with their ends even. From one end of the **outside back verticals**, measure in $8\frac{1}{2}$ inches and square a line across the boards at this point. The end from which you measured is the bottom end of the **outside back verticals**.

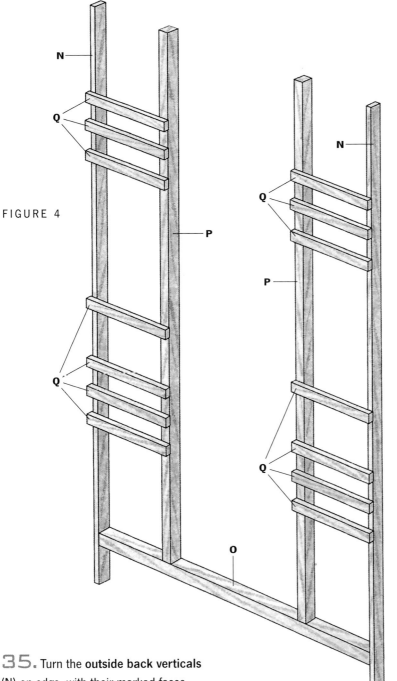

FIGURE 4

square a line across the board's inside edge at these points.

39. Cut two **inside back verticals** (P). Place one end of each **inside back vertical** against the inside edge of the **back horizontal** (O), with the outer edge of each **inside back vertical** at one of the marks from step 38. The top ends of the **inside back verticals** should be even with the top ends of the **outside back verticals**.

40. Attach the **inside back verticals** (P) by screwing through the **back horizontal** (O) into the adjoining ends of the **inside back verticals**, using one 3-inch screw at each joint.

41. Measuring down from the top ends of the **inside back verticals** (P) and the **outside back verticals** (N), square lines across all four pieces at the following points: 5 inches, 8 inches, 11 inches, 36½ inches, 42½ inches, 46 inches, and 49½ inches.

42. Cut 14 **back lattice pieces** (Q). Using Figure 4 as a guide, place the **back lattice pieces** facedown across the **inside** and **outside back verticals** (P and N), with the upper edge of each one at one of the lines from step 41. The ends of each **back lattice piece** should be flush with the outer edges of an **inside** and **outside back vertical**. Clamp the pieces in place.

43. Nail the **back lattice pieces** (Q) in place with three 3d finishing nails through each joint, using a scrap of lumber to back up the joints while you hammer. This completes the back panel.

35. Turn the **outside back verticals** (N) on edge, with their marked faces facing each other and their ends even.

36. Cut the **back horizontal** (O) and position it between the **outside back verticals** (N), with its bottom edge at the marks from step 34. The face of the **back horizontal** should be flush with the edges of the **outside back verticals**. Clamp the pieces in place.

37. Attach the **back horizontal** (O) by screwing through the **outside back verticals** (N) into the ends of the **back horizontal**, using one 3-inch screw at each joint.

38. Measure in 9¾ inches from each end of the **back horizontal** (O) and

SEAT BACK
(refer to Figure 5)

44. Cut two **seat-back end frames** (R). Refer to piece R in Figure 5. The front edges of the **seat-back end frames** are angled for better comfort, and the back edge will be installed vertically. Each **seat-back end frame** is 1¾ inches deep at its top end and 3 inches deep at its bottom end. Mark these points, draw a line between them, and cut off the waste.

45. Place the **seat-back end frames** (R) on their flat edges, parallel to each other with about 45 inches between their inside faces.

46. Cut three **seat-back slats** (S). Using Figure 5 as a guide, place the **seat-back slats** on top of the **seat-back end frames** (R), spacing them evenly. The outer edges of two of the **seat-back slats** should be flush with the ends of the **seat-back end frames**. Clamp the pieces in place. Then screw through the **seat-back slats** into the adjoining edges of the **seat-back end frames**, using two 2-inch screws at each joint. This completes the seat back.

ASSEMBLY
(refer to Figure 6)

47. You'll probably need at least one friend to help with the assembly, so go enlist one now.

48. On the inside face of each side panel (you nailed the lattice to the outside face), measure up 9 inches and 17 inches from the bottom ends of the **side verticals** (E); square a line across the boards at these points.

49. Place the side panels on edge and parallel to each other, nailed lattice sides facing out. Place the bench seat between the side panels with the outside face of the front **long seat side** (A) against the inside face of the two **side verticals** (E) that are on the ground, and the top faces of the **seat slats** (D) at the 17-inch mark you made in step 48. The **short seat sides** (B) should touch or almost touch the **long side-lattice pieces** (G) on each side panel. Clamp the panels in place.

50. Attach the side panels to the bench seat by screwing through the

front **long seat side** (A), into the adjacent faces of the **side verticals** (E), using two 2½-inch screws at each joint. (You'll need to angle the screws slightly.) Then screw through the **side verticals** that are facing up, into the adjacent ends of the **short seat sides** (B), using two 3-inch screws at each joint.

51. Stand up the side-panel/bench-seat assembly and place the bench-back assembly between the side panels, with the straight edges of the **seat-back end frames** (R) butted up against the inside faces of the two back **side verticals** (E). The 3-inch ends of the **seat-back end frames** should rest on top of the top edges of the **short seat sides** (B), and the **seat-back end frames'** faces should be flush with the faces of the **short seat sides**.

52. Attach the bench-back assembly to the side-panel/bench-seat assembly by screwing through each rear **side vertical** (E) into the adjacent edges of the **seat-back end frames** (R), using four evenly spaced 3-inch screws at each joint.

53. Lay the assembly down, back against the ground. Using Figure 6 as a guide, fit the roof assembly over the top ends of the **side verticals** (E). The inside edges of the **side verticals** should fit snugly against the outside faces of the **roof braces** (J). The top ends of the **side verticals** should extend 2 inches above the top edges of the **long roof horizontals** (I).

54. Attach the roof assembly by screwing through the inside face of each

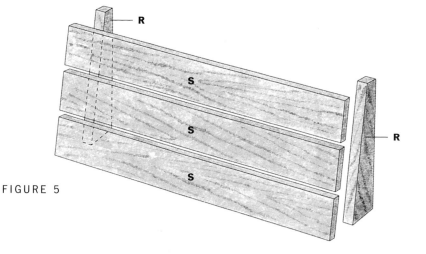

FIGURE 5

side vertical (E) into the adjoining faces of the **long roof horizontals** (I), using four 2½-inch screws at each joint.

55. Using Figure 6 as a guide, place one of the **short roof horizontals** (M) from step 33 with its outside face against the inside faces of the two front **side verticals** (E), and its bottom edge resting on the top edges of the upper **side braces** (F).

56. Attach the **short roof horizontals** (M) by screwing through their inside faces into the adjoining faces of the **side verticals** (E), using two 2½-inch screws at each joint.

57. Turn the bench-arbor so that its back is facing up. Place the back panel on top of the bench-arbor, with the top ends of the **outside** and **inside back verticals** (N and P) flush with the top edge of the **short roof horizontal** (M), and the outside faces of the **outside back verticals** against the inside edges of the **side verticals** (E).

58. Attach the back panel by screwing through the inner face of each **outside back vertical** (N) into the adjoining edges of the adjacent **side verticals** (E), using seven evenly spaced 2½-inch screws at each joint. Then screw through each **inside back vertical** (P) into the adjoining face of the adjacent **short roof horizontal** (M), using two 2½-inch screws at each joint.

59. Sand any rough edges smooth, and finish with the paint, stain, or sealer of your choice.

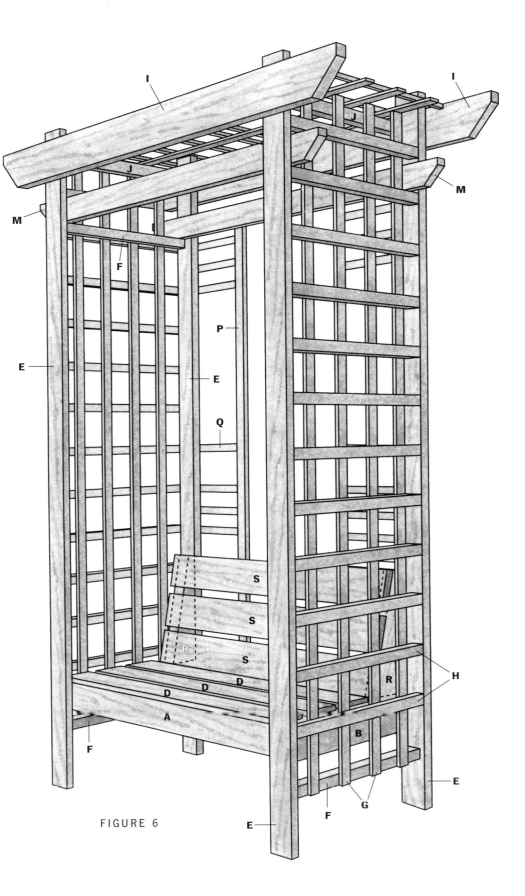

FIGURE 6

BAT ABODE

Despite their creepy reputation, bats make excellent neighbors. They're quiet and polite, and they can help eliminate all kinds of pesky insects. (One little brown bat can gobble as many as 500 mosquitoes in just one hour!) With this project's fun Gothic design, you're sure to lure at least a few of these furry flying mammals out of Transylvania and into your backyard. For tips on siting your bat abode, contact Bat Conservation International, P.O. Box 162603, Austin, TX 78716.

▼ RECOMMENDED MATERIAL

Pine or cedar for the brace (C), sides (E), and bat blocks (G); T-1-11 exterior siding for all other pieces

▼ RECOMMENDED FINISH

Flat black exterior paint for painted pieces; clear water sealer other pieces

▼ MATERIALS & SUPPLIES

$\frac{1}{2}$ piece of $\frac{3}{8}$-inch exterior siding, 4' x 4'

7 linear feet of 1 x 4 stock

2 linear feet of 1 x 2 stock

2 pieces of screen, each 12" x 16"

Clear silicone caulk

▼ HARDWARE

46 3d finish nails

20 6d finish nails

12 $\frac{3}{4}$" brads

Staples

▼ ADDITIONAL TOOLS

Miter box

Jigsaw or coping saw with a fine blade

Staple gun

▼ CUTTING LIST

CODE	DESCRIPTION	QTY	MATERIAL	DIMENSION
A	Foreground piece	1	$\frac{3}{8}$" siding	14" x 28"
B	Back piece	1	$\frac{3}{8}$" siding	14" x 28"
C	Brace	1	1 x 2 stock	18" long
D	Interior divider	1	$\frac{3}{8}$" siding	12" x 16"
E	Sides	2	1 x 4 stock	24" long
F	Front piece	1	$\frac{3}{8}$" siding	14" x 18"
G	Bat blocks	2	1 x 4 stock	14" long
H	Roof piece	1	$\frac{3}{8}$" siding	8" x 26"

INSTRUCTIONS

1. Make photocopies of Figures 1, 2, and 3 (see the following page). Then enlarge Figure 1 until it's 14 inches across and 28 inches tall. Enlarge Figure 2 until it's $12\frac{1}{2}$ inches long from nose to tail, and Figure 3 until it's $25\frac{1}{2}$ inches long and $7\frac{1}{2}$ inches wide. (You may need to cut the patterns into halves or thirds and enlarge each piece equally.)

2. Cut the **foreground piece** (A). Trace the pattern from Figure 1 onto it. Use a drill with a $1\frac{1}{4}$-inch bit to bore the circles that form the decorative "clover" shapes, centering each hole on the marks shown in Figure 1.

3. Use a drill with a $\frac{1}{4}$-inch bit to bore starter holes inside the lines of the pattern on the **foreground piece** (A). Then carefully cut out the piece's shape and the pattern using a jigsaw or a coping saw with a fine blade.

4. From the tip of the arch on the **foreground piece** (A), measure 10 inches down and mark a line across the piece's width at this point. Cut the **foreground piece** into two pieces at the line you just marked. The bottom piece will fit on top of the **front piece** (F), and the piece with the arch will fit on top of the **back piece** (B).

DESIGNER: **MARK STROM**

5. Cut the **back piece** (B); then trace the arched shape (but not the interior design) of Figure 1 onto it. Use a jigsaw or coping saw to cut the arched shape.

6. Find the center, widthwise, of the **back piece** (B) and mark a straight line along its length at this point.

7. Cut the **brace** (C). At one end, mark a 45° angle, from one corner across the face. Cut this angle using a miterbox for added precision.

8. Place the **brace** (C) on top of the **back piece** (B), centering its edge over the line you marked in step 6. The flat

end of the **brace** should be flush with the bottom end of the **back piece**, and the angle should face up (see Figure 4). Nail the brace in place with one 3d finish nail every 2 inches.

9. Cut the **interior divider** (D), and staple a 12-by-16-inch piece of screen to both sides of it; the screen will give the bat abode's residents a good surface to cling to.

10. Center the **interior divider** (D), face down, on top of the **brace** (C), bottom ends flush. Measure out from the **brace** on both sides, top and bottom, to make sure the assembly is centered and square. Then nail the **interior divider** to

the **brace**, using one 3d finish nail every 2 inches.

11. Cut two **sides** (E). Mark a 45° angle across the face of each **side** at both ends. The angles on each piece should be parallel (see E pieces in Figure 4). Cut the angles using a miter box for added precision.

12. Using Figure 4 as a guide, arrange the **sides** (E) against the **back piece** (B), with one edge of each side against the face of the **back piece**. The outside face of each **side** should be flush with one edge of the **back piece**, and the shorter angle at the bottom end of each **side** should be flush with the bottom end of

FIGURE 1

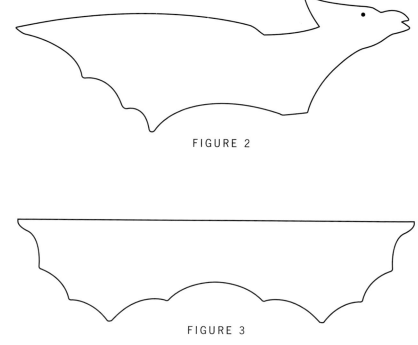

FIGURE 2

FIGURE 3

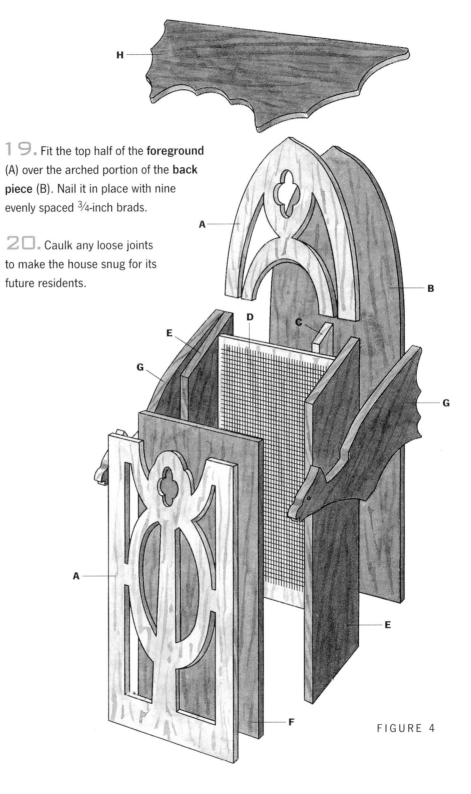

the **back piece**. Nail the **sides** into place, using one 3d finish nail every 2½".

1 3. Cut the **front piece** (F), two **bat blocks** (G), and the **roof piece** (H). Trace the pattern from Figure 2 onto each **bat block** and the pattern from Figure 3 onto the **roof piece**. Cut out the shapes using a jigsaw or a coping saw.

1 4. Paint all the pieces black except the **foreground** (A) and the **interior divider** (D). Let the paint dry.

1 5. Using Figure 4 as a guide, place the **front piece** (F) over the **sides** (E), ends even and edges flush with the outside faces of the **sides**. Nail the **front piece** in place with three evenly spaced 6d finish nails at each joint.

1 6. Fit the bottom half of the **foreground** (A) over the **front piece** (F), edges and ends even. Nail it in place with three evenly spaced 3d finish nails along each side, and three evenly spaced ¾-inch brads centered down the middle of the piece.

1 7. Using Figure 4 as a guide, nail the bats that you cut in step 13 to the sides, using four 6d finish nails per bat. The bats' top edges should be flush with the top ends of the **sides** (E).

1 8. Center the roof that you cut in step 13 over the **sides** (E) on top of the box. Attach it with three 3d finish nails along the back joint and three 6d finish nails along each side joint.

1 9. Fit the top half of the **foreground** (A) over the arched portion of the **back piece** (B). Nail it in place with nine evenly spaced ¾-inch brads.

2 0. Caulk any loose joints to make the house snug for its future residents.

FIGURE 4

DUCKBOARD SQUARE

If you're like most gardeners, you've probably experienced the frustration of trying to wash your muddy work shoes in the equally muddy spot by your garden hose. Put an end to mud-induced frustration and enhance your clean-up space with one or more simple, attractive duckboard squares. Place one by your hose to stand on while rinsing your feet, add two or three more to form a path, or use this basic concept as the first step toward creating the duckboard bench and duckboard table shown on pages 102 and 105.

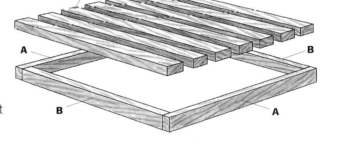

▼RECOMMENDED MATERIAL
Cypress or pressure-treated spruce or pine

▼RECOMMENDED FINISH
Clear water sealer

▼MATERIAL
16 linear feet of 1 x 2 stock

▼HARDWARE
4   1⅝" decking screws
14 1¼" decking screws

▼ADDITIONAL TOOL
Router with a ¼" roundover bit (optional)

▼CUTTING LIST

CODE	DESCRIPTION	QTY.	MATERIAL	DIMENSIONS
A	Long sides	2	1 x 2 stock	16½" long
B	Short sides	2	1 x 2 stock	15" long
C	Slats	7	1 x 2 stock	16½" long

INSTRUCTIONS

1. Cut two **long sides** (A) and two **short sides** (B).

2. On a flat surface, form a square from the **long sides** (A) and the **short sides** (B) as shown in the illustration.

3. Secure the square by screwing through the **long sides** (A) into the ends of the **short sides** (B), using one 1⅝-inch screw at each joint.

4. Cut seven **slats** (C). Use a rasp and file or a router with a roundover bit to round over the **slats'** edges.

5. Using the illustration as a guide, place the **slats** (C) on top of the square, spacing them evenly so that the outer edges of the first and last **slats** are flush with the outer faces of the **short sides** (R).

6. Screw through the **slats** (C) into the edges of the **long sides** (A), using one 1¼-inch screw at each joint.

7. Use a rasp and a file or a router with a roundover bit to round over all the exposed edges.

8. Sand the project smooth and finish as desired.

DESIGNER: **ROBIN CLARK**

POTTING BENCH

Take the mess and inconvenience out of working with potted plants with this handy and attractive potting bench. To ease construction and to create a sturdier project, we've made a few minor modifications to the designer's original potting bench. Your project will have a slightly wider bottom-shelf brace (D) and wider bottom-shelf stringers (E) than the one shown in the photo. (We made this modification to cut down on the number of rip cuts required to build the project.) It will also have carriage bolts through the frame front (H) and the frame back (I) into the narrow leg pieces (B), in addition to the ones through the frame sides (F) into the wide leg pieces (A).

▼ RECOMMENDED MATERIAL

Cedar or pine

▼ RECOMMENDED FINISH

Clear water sealer or exterior stain

▼ MATERIALS

35 linear feet of 1 x 4 stock
38 linear feet of 1 x 6 stock
13 linear feet of 1 x 2 stock

▼ HARDWARE

16   2" decking screws
102 1⅝" decking screws
12   ¼" x 2" carriage bolts
12   ¼" washers
12   ¼" nuts
20   1¼" decking screws
Screw hooks (optional)

▼ ADDITIONAL TOOL

Hand plane

▼ CUTTING LIST

CODE	DESCRIPTION	QTY.	MATERIAL	DIMENSIONS
A	Wide leg pieces	4	1 x 4 stock	3" x 35"
B	Narrow leg pieces	4	1 x 4 stock	2¼" x 35"
C	Bottom-shelf slats	4	1 x 6 stock	4½" x 32½"
D	Bottom-shelf brace	1	1 x 4 stock	16" long
E	Bottom-shelf stringers	2	1 x 4 stock	18" long
F	Frame sides	2	1 x 6 stock	21" long
G	Frame-side braces	2	1 x 2 stock	11" long
H	Frame front	1	1 x 4 stock	2½" x 34"
I	Frame back	1	1 x 6 stock	34" long
J	Wide work-surface slats	2	1 x 6 stock	34" long
K	Narrow work-surface slats	2	1 x 6 stock	5" x 24"
L	Frame stringers	4	1 x 2 stock	19⅜" long
M	Dirt-drop slats	2	1 x 6 stock	5" x 10"
N	Dirt-drop braces	2	1 x 2 stock	9½" long
O	Shelf supports	2	1 x 6 stock	16" long
P	Shelf rests	2	1 x 2 stock	5½" long
Q	Shelf	1	1 x 6 stock	32½" long
R	Shelf back	1	1 x 4 stock	34" long

INSTRUCTIONS

1. Cut four **wide leg pieces** (A) and four **narrow leg pieces** (B).

2. To assemble a leg, place a **wide leg piece** (A) against a **narrow leg piece** (B), as shown in the illustration on page 73. The edge of the **wide leg piece** should be flush with the face of the **narrow leg piece**, and their ends should be even. Clamp the pieces in place. Screw through the **wide leg piece** into the edge of the **narrow leg piece**, using five evenly spaced 1⅝-inch screws.

3. Repeat step 2 three times to assemble the other three legs.

4. Cut four **bottom-shelf slats** (C).

5. Lay out the **bottom-shelf slats** (C) facedown and edge to edge, with their ends even. Clamp the boards in place. From both ends of each board, measure in 15⅞ inches and mark these points across all four **bottom-shelf slats**. This will give you two lines, ¾ inch apart, at the middle of the **bottom-shelf slats**. You'll use these lines to place the **bottom-shelf brace** (D) in step 8.

6. Cut the **bottom-shelf brace** (D) and two **bottom-shelf stringers** (E).

7. Lay out the **bottom-shelf stringers** (E), on edge and parallel, about 32½ inches apart. Place the **bottom-shelf brace** (D) on edge between the **bottom-shelf stringers**.

8. Place the clamped **bottom-shelf slats** (C) on top of the **bottom-shelf stringers** (E) and the **bottom-shelf brace** (D). The ends of the **bottom-shelf slats** should be flush with the outside faces of the **bottom-shelf stringers**, and the **bottom-shelf brace** should be directly between the lines you marked in step 5; the length of the **bottom-shelf brace** should be centered across the width of the clamped **bottom-shelf slats**. Clamp the pieces in place.

9. Screw through the **bottom-shelf slats** (C) into the adjoining edges of the **bottom-shelf stringers** (E), using two 1⅝-inch screws at each joint. Then screw through the **bottom-shelf slats** into the edge of each **bottom-shelf stringer**, using one 1⅝-inch screw at

each joint. This completes the bottom-shelf assembly.

10. As you can see in the illustration, the bottom shelf fits inside the legs, with the outside faces of the **bottom-shelf stringers** (E) against the inside faces of the **wide leg pieces** (A). The bottom shelf is attached to the legs with ¼-inch x 2-inch bolts through the **wide leg pieces**, into the adjacent **bottom-shelf stringers**. You'll need to bore matching ¼-inch holes through the **bottom-shelf stringers** and the adjacent **wide leg pieces** to accommodate the bolts; do this by measuring and marking, on the inside, 12¾ inches up from the bottom of each leg.

11. Position the bottom-shelf assembly on end, and position the leg so that the bottom edge of the **bottom-shelf stringer** (E) is on the 12¾-inch mark and the leg is tight against the corner of the shelf assembly. Clamp the pieces and bore a ¼-inch hole through the **wide leg pieces** (A) and through the adjacent **bottom-shelf stringer**. Repeat for each leg assembly. Then secure the pieces with ¼-inch x 2-inch bolts, washers, and nuts.

12. Cut two **frame sides** (F).

13. Refer to piece F in the illustration. To mark the angle at the front end of each **frame side** (F), start by measuring 2¼ inches down from one edge. Mark this point on the end of the board. Repeat with the other **frame side**.

14. Starting from the same end that you marked in step 13, measure in 2¼

inches and mark this point on the top edge of the **frame side** (F). Repeat with the other **frame side**.

15. Draw straight lines to connect the marks from steps 13 and 14. Cut the **frame sides'** (F) angles along these lines.

16. Designate one **frame side** (F) "right" and one "left"; this is to determine which face is the "inside" face for attaching the **frame-side braces** (G) in step 19.

17. On the inside face of each **frame side** (F), measure up 1 inch from the bottom edge and mark a line across the length of the board at this point. You'll use this line to position the **frame-side braces** (G) in step 19.

18. Cut two **frame-side braces** (G).

19. Center a **frame-side brace** (G) face-to-face against a **frame side** (F), with its bottom edge at the line that you marked in step 17. Screw through the **frame-side brace** into the **frame side**, using three 1¼-inch screws. Repeat with the remaining **frame side** and **frame-side brace**.

20. Cut the **frame front** (H) and the **frame back** (I).

21. Using the illustration as a guide, place the **frame front** (H) between the angled ends of the **frame sides** (F). The bottom edge of the **frame front** should be flush with the bottom edges of the **frame sides**. Place the **frame back** (I)

between the opposite ends of the **frame sides**. Check for squareness and clamp the pieces in place. Screw through the **frame sides** into the adjacent ends of the **frame front** and the **frame back**, using two 2-inch screws at each joint. This will form the frame.

22. Cut two **wide work-surface slats** (J) and two **narrow work-surface slats** (K).

23. Cut 10 inches off one end of each **narrow work surface slat** (K) and save these 10-inch pieces until step 33 to make the cover for the dirt drop; they are the **dirt-drop slats** (M).

24. Lay out the **narrow work-surface slats** (K) edge to edge with their ends even. Place a **wide work-surface slat** (J) edge to edge against the outside of both **narrow work-surface slats**. The ends of all the boards should be even at one end; at the other end, the boards of the same length should be even. Clamp the boards in place.

25. From both ends of the **wide work-surface slats** (J), measure in 9½ inches and mark these points across all four boards. These lines will show you where to place the frame-stringer assembly in step 28.

26. Cut four **frame stringers** (L).

27. As you can see in the illustration, the **frame stringers** (L) are attached to one another in pairs. Using the illustration as a guide, position one **frame stringer**, face flush to the edge of

another **frame stringer**, with their ends even. Clamp the pieces in place. Then screw through the face of the first **frame stringer** into the edge of the second one, using three evenly spaced 1¼-inch screws. Repeat with the remaining two **frame stringers**.

28. Place a frame-stringer assembly across the work-surface assembly inside each line that you marked in step 25. Screw through the **frame stringers** (L) that are against the **work-surface slats** (K and J), using two 1¼-inch screws at each **work-surface slat**. This completes the work-surface assembly.

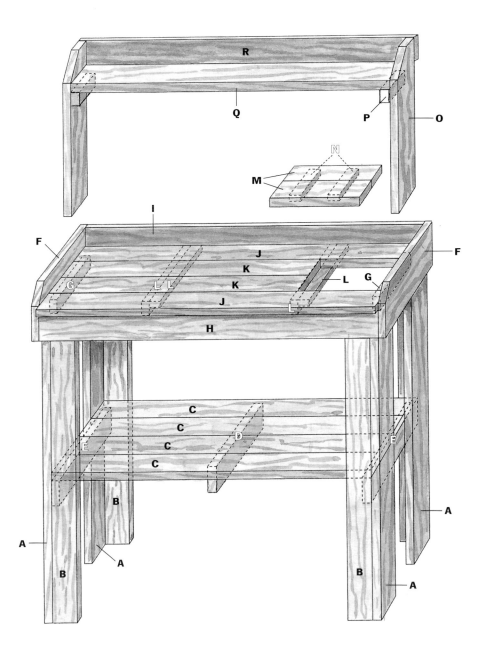

29. Place the work-surface assembly on top of the frame. To hold the work-surface assembly even, place a 2½-inch-high scrap of lumber under the work-surface assembly, at the edge that's against the **frame back** (I). The front edge of the work surface will overlap the **frame front** (H) by ¾ inch, and the back edge of the work-surface assembly should butt up against the inside face of the **frame back**. Clamp the pieces in place.

30. Screw through the **frame front** (H) and the **frame back** (I) into the adjacent ends of the **frame stringers** (L), using one 1¼-inch screw at each joint.

31. Fit the assembly you just completed over the legs and clamp it in place.

32. Bore a ¼-inch hole through the **frame front** (H), through each adjacent **narrow leg piece** (B). Then bore a ¼-inch hole through the **frame back** (I), through each adjacent **narrow leg piece**. Attach the pieces with ¼-inch x 2-inch bolts through these holes. Secure each bolt with a washer and a nut.

33. To build the cover for the dirt drop—the space between the ends of the **narrow work-surface slats** (K) and one **frame side** (F)—start by placing the two 10-inch **dirt-drop slats** (M) from step 23 together, edge to edge, with their ends even. Measure in 2 inches from both ends of both **dirt-drop slats** and mark these points across the boards. These lines will show you where to place the **dirt-drop braces** (N) in step 35.

34. Cut two **dirt-drop braces** (N).

35. Place a **dirt-drop brace** (N) facedown across the **dirt-drop slats** (M) inside each line you marked in step 33. The ends of the **dirt-drop braces** should be ¼ inch from the outside edges of the **dirt-drop slats**. Screw through the **dirt-drop braces** into the **dirt-drop slats**, using two 1¼-inch screws for each brace. You may need to plane a little off the sides of this assembly so that it fits into the work surface.

36. To make the top shelf, start by cutting two **shelf supports** (O).

37. Mark and cut an angle at one end of each **shelf support** (O), following the same technique described in steps 13–15.

38. Measure 11½ inches up from the bottom end (the end without the angle) of each **shelf support** (O) and mark a line across the width of each board at these points. These lines will show you where to place the **shelf rests** (P) in step 40.

39. Cut two **shelf rests** (P).

40. On each **shelf support** (O), place a **shelf rest** (P) with its lower edge at the line that you marked in step 38. The ends of the **shelf rest** should be flush with the edges of the **shelf support**. Screw through the **shelf rests** into the **shelf supports**, using two 1¼-inch screws at each joint.

41. Cut the **shelf** (Q).

42. Using the illustration as a guide, place the **shelf** (Q) on top of the top edges of the **shelf rests** (P). The edges of the **shelf** should be flush with the ends of the **shelf rests**. Screw through the **shelf** into the edges of the **shelf rests**, using two 1¼-inch screws at each joint.

43. Cut the **shelf back** (R).

44. Using the illustration as a guide, position the **shelf back** (R) against the rear edges of the **shelf supports** (O). The top edge of the **shelf back** should be flush with the top ends of the **shelf supports**. Clamp the pieces in place. Then screw through the **shelf back** into the edges of the **shelf supports**, using two 1¼-inch screws at each joint.

45. If you'd like to hang tools from your potting bench, as shown in the photo on the title page, attach screw hooks to the underside of the **shelf** (Q).

46. Place the top shelf assembly inside the frame of the work surface assembly, with the rear edges of the **shelf supports** (O) fitted snugly against the inside face of the **frame back** (I). Screw through the **shelf supports** into the **frame sides** (F), using two 1¼-inch screws at each joint.

47. Sand the entire piece smooth; then finish with a waterproof sealer or stain.

GARDEN TOTE

Lugging armfuls of spades, hand rakes, and seed packets back and forth from row to row can make gardening seem more like work than fun. With this garden tote, though, you can transport all your gardening necessities in one easy trip. And unlike its mass-produced counterparts, this project is attractive enough to use indoors as well as out.

DESIGNER: **ROBIN CLARK**

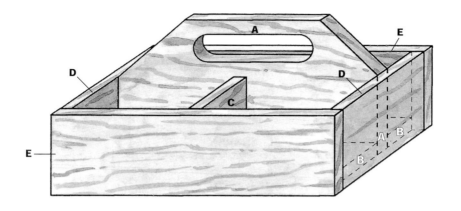

▼ **RECOMMENDED MATERIAL**

Cedar or pine

▼ **RECOMMENDED FINISH**

Clear water sealer

▼ **MATERIALS**

1½ linear feet of 1 x 8 stock

9 linear feet of 1 x 6 stock

▼ **HARDWARE**

36 1½" decking screws

▼ **ADDITIONAL TOOL**

Router with ¼" roundover bit

   (optional)

▼ **CUTTING LIST**

CODE	DESCRIPTION	QTY.	MATERIAL	DIMENSIONS
A	Handle	1	1 x 8 stock	14½" long
B	Floor pieces	2	1 x 6 stock	14½" long
C	Divider	1	1 x 6 stock	3¼" long
D	Ends	2	1 x 6 stock	4" x 11¾"
E	Sides	2	1 x 6 stock	4" x 16"

INSTRUCTIONS

1. Cut the **handle** (A).

2. To make the oblong opening in the **handle** (A), start by measuring down 1 inch from one edge of the **handle**; mark this point along the length of the board. This will be the **handle's** top edge.

3. Measure down 2½ inches from the top edge of the **handle** (A) and mark this point along the length of the board.

4. Measure in 3¾ inches from both ends of the **handle** (A) and square this point across the width of the board.

5. The rectangle formed by the lines from steps 2, 3, and 4 marks the area where you'll cut the oblong **handle** (A) opening. Use a drill with a 1½-inch spade bit to bore a series of connecting holes through the **handle**, inside the rectangle. Smooth the edges of the opening with a rasp and finish with sandpaper.

6. At the top edge of the **handle** (A), measure in 3¼ inches from each end and mark these points.

7. From the top edge of the **handle** (A), measure 3 inches down on each end and mark these points.

8. At both corners of the top edge of the **handle** (A), connect the points from steps 6 and 7 with a straight line. Cut the angles at both ends of the **handle** to these lines.

9. Sand the top edge and the angles of the **handle** (A) smooth.

10. Cut two **floor pieces** (B).

11. Place the edge of one **floor piece** (B) against one face of the **handle** (A), along the **handle's** bottom edge, as shown in the illustration. Screw through the **handle** into the edge of the **floor piece**, with one 1½-inch screw located about 2 inches off the **handle's** center, widthwise. The **floor piece** should swivel on the screw.

12. Attach the second **floor piece** (B) to the other face of the **handle** (A), locating its screw about 2 inches off-center in the opposite direction from the screw attaching the first **floor piece**.

13. Cut the **divider** (C), and sand one of its edges smooth; this will be the **divider's** top edge.

14. Center one end of the **divider** (C) against one face of the **handle** (A). Screw through the **handle** into the end of the **divider**, using two 1½-inch screws.

15. Cut two 11¾-inch lengths from 1 x 6 stock. Rip two 4-inch-wide **ends** (D) from these lengths.

16. Place an **end** (D) against one end of the floor-handle assembly, with its bottom edge flush with the bottom face of the **floor pieces** (B). Screw through the **end** into the ends of the **floor pieces**, using two 1½-inch screws for each **floor piece**. Then screw through the **end** into the end of the **handle** with two 1½-inch screws.

17. Repeat step 16 with the remaining **end** (D) at the other end of the floor-handle assembly.

18. Cut two 16-inch lengths from 1 x 6 stock. Rip the two 4-inch-wide **sides** (E) from these lengths.

19. Position a **side** (E) against one edge of the floor-handle assembly, with its bottom edge flush with the bottom face of the adjacent **floor piece** (B). The **side's** ends should be flush with the outer faces of the **ends** (D).

20. Screw through the **side** (E) into the edge of the **floor piece** (B), using four evenly spaced 1½-inch screws. Then screw through the **side** into the ends of the **divider** (C) and the **ends** (D), using two 1½-inch screws at each joint.

21. Repeat step 20 to attach the other **side** (E) to the other side of the tool tote.

22. Sand any rough edges smooth and finish as desired.

DESIGNER: **BARRY TRIBBLE**

WALL-MOUNTED TOOL HOLDER

If you spend more time searching for your spade than sowing seeds, it might be time for you to impose some order in your garden shed. This ingenious tool holder will organize your garden implements and stretch your storage space at the same time. Pegs and shelves made from "1 x" lumber and held in place by the force of friction adjust side to side and up and down to accommodate a variety of tool sizes and shapes. This project is so handy and so easy to build that you might find yourself making an extra one for the kitchen!

▼ **RECOMMENDED MATERIAL**

Pressure-treated pine or spruce

▼ **RECOMMENDED FINISH**

Clear water sealer or exterior paint

▼ **MATERIALS AND SUPPLIES**

51 linear feet of 1 x 2 PT stock

12 or more linear feet of 1 x 1 PT stock (The actual amount will depend on the number of 6"-long pegs (C) you want to cut.)

12 or more linear feet of 1 x 6 PT stock (The actual amount will depend on the number and length of shelves (D) you want to cut.)

▼ **HARDWARE**

30 $1\frac{1}{4}$" decking screws

8 $1\frac{1}{2}$" decking screws

▼ **CUTTING LIST**

CODE	DESCRIPTION	QTY.	MATERIAL	DIMENSIONS
A	Verticals	3	1 x 2 PT stock	$37\frac{1}{2}$" long
B	Horizontals	10	1 x 2 PT stock	48" long
C	Pegs	As many as desired	1 x 1 PT stock	6" long
D	Shelves	As many as desired	1 x 6 PT stock	Up to $22\frac{3}{4}$" long

INSTRUCTIONS

1. Cut three **verticals** (A) and ten **horizontals** (B).

2. Lay out the **horizontals** (B), facedown and edge to edge, with their ends even. From both ends of each **horizontal**, measure in $23\frac{5}{8}$ inches and mark these points across the face of all ten boards. This will give you two lines, $\frac{3}{4}$ inch apart in the middle of each **horizontal**; these lines will show you how to position the **horizontals** over the middle **vertical** (A) in step 4.

3. Lay out the **verticals** (A) on edge, with their ends even. From the same end on each **vertical**, measure in and mark the following points across the

edge of each board: $2\frac{1}{4}$ inches, $11\frac{1}{4}$ inches, $19\frac{1}{4}$ inches, $27\frac{1}{4}$ inches, and $36\frac{1}{4}$ inches. These lines will show you where to place the **horizontals** (B) in the next step.

4. Using the illustration on the next page as a guide, place a **horizontal** (B) facedown across the **verticals** (A), below each of the five lines that you marked in step 3. The middle **vertical** should fit directly between the lines you marked in step 2 (this will ensure that the piece is centered properly), and the ends of the **horizontals** should be flush with the outside faces of the two outermost **verticals**. Clamp the pieces in place.

5. Screw through each **horizontal** (B), into the adjoining edges of the **verticals**

(A), using one 1-¼-inch screw at each joint. This is the front side of the tool holder.

6. Turn the assembly over.

7. Working from the same end as in step 3, measure down and mark the following points across the edge of each **vertical** (A): 9 inches, 17 inches, 25 inches, and 34 inches. These lines will show you where to place the **horizontals** (B) in the next step.

8. Place one **horizontal** (B) with its upper edge flush with the ends of the **verticals** (A) from which you measured in step 7. Place the four remaining **horizontals** below each of the lines that you made in step 7. Attach the pieces with a 1¼-inch screw at each joint.

9. Cut several **pegs** (C).

10. Cut several **shelves** (D) of various lengths.

11. Sand the ends of the **pegs** (C) and the **shelves** (D), but not the edges; these pieces depend on gravity and friction to hold them in place on the tool holder.

12. Paint or finish the tool holder, **pegs** (C), and **shelves** (D) as desired.

13. Mount the project, front side out, with four evenly spaced 1½-inch screws through the top and bottom **horizontals** (B).

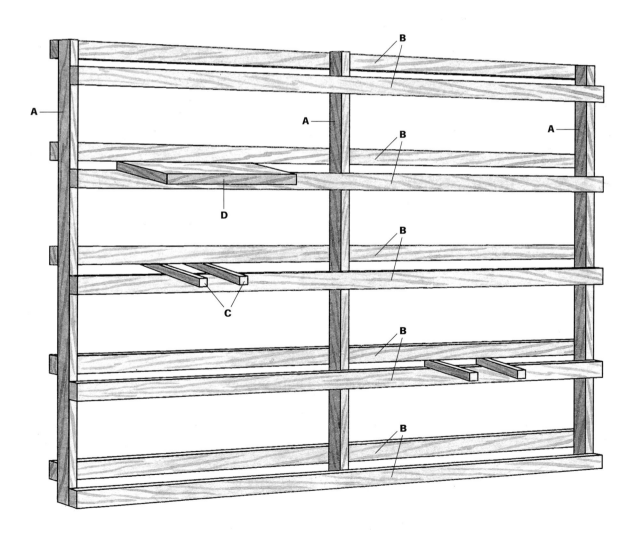

COMPOST BIN

As landfill space becomes scarce and costly, composting is more and more *the* way to recycle yard and kitchen waste. This sturdy and—yes!—attractive two-bin composting system allows you to accumulate materials in one container while storing aged, aerated, ready-to-spread mulch in the other. Removable slats on the front panels give you and your shovel easy access to either pile.

DESIGNER: **JIM HOWE**

Pressure-treated pine or spruce for the base rails (A) and base joists (B), and cedar or pine for all other pieces

▼ RECOMMENDED FINISH

Water sealer

▼ MATERIALS

26 linear feet of 2 x 4 PT stock
36 linear feet of 2 x 4 stock
20 linear feet of 2 x 6 stock
180 linear feet of 1 x 6 stock

▼ HARDWARE

120 10d spiral siding nails
80 16d ring shank nails
24 1½" wood screws (These screws will hold the strap hinges in place, so the gauge number must fit into the holes in the hinges you purchase.)
16 2" decking screws
188 1⅝" decking screws
54 1¼" decking screws
4 5" galvanized strap hinges with accompanying hardware
12 ¼" x 3½" carriage bolts
12 ¼" nuts
12 ¼" flat washers

▼ ADDITIONAL TOOLS

Circular saw with a rip fence
Framing square
Socket wrench and ⅜" socket
Scrap of cardboard
Help from at least one friend

▼ CUTTING LIST

CODE	DESCRIPTION	QTY.	MATERIAL	DIMENSIONS
A	Base rails	2	2 x 4 PT stock	68" long
B	Base joists	5	2 x 4 PT stock	30" long
C	Floorboards	6	1 x 6 stock	5" x 68"
D	Wide leg pieces	4	2 x 6 stock	35½" long
E	Narrow leg pieces	4	2 x 4 stock	35½" long
F	Wide mid-post pieces	2	2 x 6 stock	31¼" long
G	Narrow mid-post piece	2	2 x 4 stock	35½" long
H	Back slats	15	1 x 6 stock	31⅜" long
I	Side slats	10	1 x 6 stock	33¼" long
J	Front slat stop	1	1 x 6 stock	33⅛" long
K	Front slats	1	1 x 6 stock	1½" x 24"
L	Lid slats	12	1 x 6 stock	36" long
M	Lid battens	4	1 x 6 stock	2⅝" x 29½"
N	Hinge blocks	4	2 x 4 stock	5" long
O	Front base trim blocks	2	2 x 4 stock	30¼" long
P	Rear base trim blocks	2	2 x 4 stock	30¼" long
Q	Side base trim blocks	2	2 x 4 stock	22" long
R	Lid-support arms	2	1 x 6 stock	1½" x 24"
S	Lid-support arm blocks	2	1 x 6 stock	1½" x 2"

INSTRUCTIONS

1. Cut two base rails (A) and five base joists (B).

2. Place the base rails (A) together, edge to edge with their ends even. Measuring from one end, mark points along the length of each base rail at 17-inch intervals; you'll make a total of three marks on each base rail, dividing the boards into four equal sections.

3. At each mark that you made in step 2, measure over (along the board's length) ¾ inch to each side and square lines across the base rails' (A) widths at these points.

4. Turn the base rails (A) on edge, with their marked faces toward each other. Using the illustration on page 84 as a guide, position a base joist (B) on edge between the base rails, inside each set of lines that you marked in step 3. Then place a base joist between each set of the base rails' ends. The outer faces of these last two base joists should be flush with the base rails' ends and the top edges of all the base joists should be flush with the top edges of the base rails. Clamp the pieces in place.

5. Attach the base rails (A) to the base joists (B) by driving two 16d ring shank nails through the base rails into each adjoining base joist end.

6. Cut six 68-inch lengths from 1 x 6 stock. Rip the six 5-inch-wide **floorboards** (C) from these lengths.

7. Using the illustration as a guide, place the **floorboards** (C) facedown across the **base joists** (B), spacing the boards evenly (about ⅝ inch between edges). The outer edges of the outermost **floorboards** should be flush with the outside faces of the **base rails** (A).

8. Attach the pieces with two 10d spiral siding nails through the **floorboards** (C), and into the edge of each adjoining **base joist** (B). This completes the compost bin's base.

9. Cut four **wide leg pieces** (D) and four **narrow leg pieces** (E).

10. Form an L-shape with one **wide leg piece** (D) and one **narrow leg piece** (E) by butting the edge of the **wide leg piece** against the face of the **narrow leg piece**. The **wide leg piece's** face should be flush with one of the **narrow leg piece's** edges, and the ends of both pieces should be even. Attach the pieces with five evenly spaced 16d ring shank nails through the **narrow leg piece's** face, into the **wide leg piece's** edge.

11. Repeat step 10 three times to build the remaining leg assemblies.

12. Cut two **wide mid-post pieces** (F) and two **narrow mid-post pieces** (G).

13. Form a T-shape with one **wide mid-post piece** (F) and one **narrow mid-post piece** (G) by centering the edge of the **wide mid-post piece** over the face of

the **narrow mid-post piece**. The pieces' ends should be even at one end; this is the top end of the mid-post assembly. Attach the pieces with five evenly spaced 16d ring shank nails through the face of the **narrow mid-post piece** into the edge of the **wide mid-post piece**.

14. Repeat step 13 to build the second mid-post assembly.

15. Place a leg assembly, **narrow leg piece** (E) facedown, and a mid-post assembly, **narrow mid-post piece** (G) facedown, on a flat work surface. The ends of the assemblies should be even and the leg assembly's angle should be facing the mid-post assembly.

16. Cut ten **back slats** (H).

17. Using the illustration as a guide, place a **back slat** (H), facedown, between the leg assembly and the mid-post assembly, top edge flush with the assemblies' top ends. On the leg-assembly side, the **back slat's** end should butt up against the inside face of the **wide leg piece** (D); on the mid-post assembly side, the **back slat's** end should butt up against the inside face of the **wide mid-post piece** (F).

18. Screw through the **back slat** (H) into the adjoining faces of the **narrow leg piece** (E) and the **narrow mid-post piece** (G), using two 1⅝-inch screws at each joint.

19. Attach four more **back slats** (H) under the first one, using a scrap of 1 x as a ¾-inch spacer between the pieces.

There should be at least 4¾ inches between the bottom edge of the fifth **back slat** and the bottom ends of the leg assembly and mid-post assembly. This completes half of the back panel.

20. To complete the back panel, place a second leg assembly, **narrow leg piece** (E) facedown and angle pointing in, on the other side of the mid-post assembly. Repeat steps 17–19 to attach **back slats** (H) to this side of the back panel. This completes the back panel.

21. Grab a friend to help with the next few steps.

22. Position the back panel against one long side of the base. The **back slats** (H) should be parallel to one **base rail** (A), and the outer faces of the outermost **base joists** (B) should fit snug against the inside faces of the **wide leg pieces** (D).

23. To temporarily secure the back panel to the base, drive two 10d spiral siding nails through each **narrow leg piece** (E) and the **narrow mid-post piece** (G), into the adjoining **base rail** (A). (Use a framing square to assure that the back is perpendicular to the floor.) Then drive two 10d spiral siding nails through each **wide leg piece** (D) into the adjoining **base joist** (B).

24. Fit a leg assembly against both of the remaining corners on the base. As in step 22, the outer faces of the outermost **base joists** (B) should fit snugly against the inside faces of the **wide leg pieces** (D). Temporarily secure the

pieces with two 10d spiral siding nails through each **narrow leg piece** (E) into the adjoining **base rail** (A), and two 10d spiral siding nails through each **wide leg piece** into the adjoining **base joist**. (Use a framing square to make sure that the legs are perpendicular to the floor in both directions.)

25. Position the remaining mid-post assembly at the front of the compost bin, directly opposite the mid-post assembly in the back panel. Make sure it is square to the floor; then temporarily secure it in place with two 10d spiral siding nails through the **narrow mid-post piece** (G) into the face of the adjoining **base rail** (A).

26. Bore two ¼-inch holes through each **wide leg piece** (D), and through the adjoining **base joists** (B). Then bore two ¼-inch holes through each **narrow mid-post piece** (G), through the adjoining **base rail** (A). Secure the pieces with a 3½-inch carriage bolt through each of these holes.

27. Cut fifteen **side slats** (I).

28. Fit a **side slat** (I) inside two leg assemblies, with its top edge flush with the leg assemblies' top ends. The **side slat's** rear end should butt up against the face of the adjoining **back slat** (H). The other end should be at least ¾ inch from the inside face of the **narrow leg piece** (E) at the front of the box. (This distance will vary based on the actual thickness of your wood.) Screw through the **side slat** into the adjoining **wide leg pieces** (D), using two 1⅝-inch screws at each joint.

29. Attach four more **side slats** (I) under the first one, using a scrap of 1 x as a ¾-inch spacer between the pieces.

30. Repeat steps 28–29 on the other side of the compost bin.

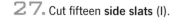

31. Attach the remaining five **side slats** (I) to one side of the mid-post assemblies the same way you attached the **side slats** to the leg assemblies in steps 28–29. (It doesn't matter to which side of the mid-post assemblies you attach the **side slats**.)

32. On the **wide mid-post piece** (F) at the front of the compost bin, measure $3/4$ inch in from the piece's front edge (this distance will vary based on your wood's actual thickness). Mark this point along the length of the board on the face to which the **side slats** (I) aren't attached.

33. Cut the **front slat stop** (J). Place it, face-to-face and edges parallel, against the **wide mid-post piece** (F), front edge on the line you marked in step 32. Screw through the **front slat stop** into the **wide mid-post piece**, using four evenly spaced $1^5/8$-inch screws.

34. Cut ten **front slats** (K). On each one, drive two $1^5/8$-inch screws into the thickness of one edge, locating the screws about 1 inch in from each end, and leaving about $3/4$ inch of the screws' length protruding. The protruding screws will act as $3/4$-inch spacers when the **front slats** are in position.

35. Slide five **front slats** (K), screw-edge down, into the space between the **front slat stop** (J) and the **narrow mid-post piece** (G). Slide the remaining **front slats** into place on the other side of the compost bin's front.

36. Cut twelve **lid slats** (L).

37. Cut two $29^1/2$-inch lengths from 1 x 6 stock. Rip two $2^5/8$-inch **lid battens** (M) from each length.

38. Lay six **lid slats** (L) on a flat work surface, edge to edge and ends even. Measure in $3^1/2$ inches from each end of the **lid slats** and mark these points across all six boards. Then measure in $3^1/2$ inches from the outer edge of the two outermost **lid slats** and mark this point along the length of these boards. These lines mark where you'll place the **lid battens** (M).

39. Use a scrap of 1 x material to space the **lid slats** (L) $3/4$ inch apart, making sure that the boards' ends stay even. Place a **lid batten** (M) across the **lid slats**, inside each set of lines from step 38. Screw through each **lid batten** into the adjoining **lid slat**, using two $1^1/4$-inch screws at each **lid slat**. This completes the first lid unit.

40. Repeat steps 38–39 to build the second lid unit.

41. At the back of the compost bin, measure 2 inches over from both edges of the **narrow mid-post piece** (G) and mark these points across the width of the outside faces of the adjoining top **back slats** (H).

42. Cut four **hinge blocks** (N). Place a **hinge block** face-to-face, against each **back slat** (H) that you marked in step 41, top end flush with the top edge of the adjoining **back slat** (H), and inside edge against the 2-inch line. Clamp the pieces in place. Screw through the inside face of each **back slat** into the adjoining **hinge block**, using four 2-inch screws for each **hinge block**. You'll attach two **hinge blocks** in this step.

43. Butt the edge of one of the remaining **hinge blocks** (N) against the inside edge of one of the rear **wide leg pieces** (D), face to face and top end even with the top edge of the top **back slat** (H). Screw through the inside face of the **back slat**, into the **hinge block**, using four 2-inch screws.

44. Repeat step 43 with the last **hinge block** (N) at the other rear **wide leg piece** (D).

45. Place the two lid units in place on top of the compost bin, with the back edge—the outer edge of the rear **lid slat** (L)—of each lid unit even with the outside face of the rear **wide leg pieces** (D) and **narrow mid-post piece** (G). The lids should overhang about 1 inch at each side of the compost bin and about $3/4$ inch at the front. Leave a $1/8$-inch gap between the two lids.

46. Slip a piece of cardboard under the backs of the lids to leave a clearance of about $1/16$ inch. Using the $1^1/2$-inch wood screws and remembering to bore appropriately sized pilot holes first, attach the hinges to the lid units, centering the hinges on the **lid battens** (M) under the **lid slats** (L). Be sure that the screws go through the **lid slats** into the adjoining **lid battens**.

47. Keeping the lids in place, attach the hinges to the **hinge blocks** (N) with 1½-inch wood screws. (Note that the top two holes in the portion of the hinge that attaches to the **hinge blocks** will not be over wood.)

48. Cut two **front base trim blocks** (O). Position the **front base trim blocks** against the front of the compost bin's base, placing one between each front leg assembly and the mid-post assembly, face against the front **base rail** (A). Attach the pieces with six 10d spiral siding nails, spacing them evenly along the length of the **front base trim blocks**.

49. Cut two **rear base trim blocks** (P) and attach them to the back of the compost bin the same way you attached the **front base trim blocks** (O) in step 48.

50. Cut two **side base trim blocks** (Q) and attach them to the sides of the compost bin's base, using the same method as in step 48. (Note that the face of each **side base trim block** will be against an outside **base joist** (B), rather than a **base rail** (A), as in step 48.)

51. Cut a 30-inch length from a piece of 1 x 6 stock; then rip two 1½-inch-wide pieces from this piece. Cut a **lid-support arm** (R) from each of the two resulting pieces. Cut two **lid-support arm blocks** (S) from the remaining pieces (set these aside until step 56).

52. Bore a ³⁄₁₆-inch hole through each **lid-support arm** (R), locating the hole about ¾ inch from one end and centering it widthwise. This size hole will allow the **lid-support arm** to rotate on the screw when you attach it to the side assembly in step 56.

53. Measure 6 inches in from the outside face of the front **narrow mid-post piece** (G) and mark this point on the attached **wide mid-post piece** (F) and on the opposite face of the adjacent top **side slat** (I). Then measure 1 inch down from the top edges of the **wide mid-post piece** and the top **side slat** and mark these points across the 6-inch marks that you just made. The intersection of the 1-inch and 6-inch marks shows where to attach the **lid-support arms** (R) in the next step.

54. Position a **lid-support arm** (R) against the **wide mid-post piece** (G) that you marked in step 53 so that the hole you bored in step 52 is directly over the point you marked in step 53. Attach the **lid-support arm** with a 1⅝-inch screw through the hole. Attach the other **lid-support arm** to the top **side slat** that you marked in step 53 the same way.

55. From the point where you attached each **lid-support arm** (R), measure straight back about 23½ inches and mark this point on the rear **wide mid-post piece** (F) and on the same face of the same **side slat** (I) that you marked in step 53. Measure down 1½ inches from the top edges of the **wide mid-post piece** and the **side slat** and mark these points across the 23½-inch marks. The intersections of the 23½-inch marks and the 1½-inch marks show where to attach the **lid-support arm blocks** (S) in the next step.

56. Position a **lid-support arm block** (S) against the **wide mid-post piece** (G) that you marked in step 55, with its upper edge at the point you marked. Screw through the **lid-support arm block** into the **wide mid-post piece** using a 1¼-inch screw. Then attach the remaining **lid-support arm block** to the **side slate** the same way. These blocks will keep the **lid-support arms** (R) from falling into the compost.

57. Sand all of the compost bin's exposed edges and ends smooth.

58. If you used cedar and pressure-treated wood to build this project, it will be naturally weather resistant. However, a minimum of two coats of a high-quality water sealer will keep your compost bin looking new and will offer added protection against rot and weather damage. Just be sure to check that the water sealer is non-toxic, in case it leaches into your compost.

SEEDLING TRAYS

Forget those floppy, flimsy, use-'em-once-and-throw-'em-away plastic seedling trays. In less time than it takes to run to the greenhouse and back, you can build these sturdy-yet-stunning, use-'em-for-years versions. To build the smaller seedling tray shown in the project photo and in Figure 1, use the first Materials and Hardware lists and the first Cutting List. To build the larger tray shown in the photo, use the second Materials and Hardware lists and the second Cutting List. The directions for building both tray sizes are almost identical. (The only differences are noted in steps 2 and 5.)

DESIGNER: **JOE ARCHIBALD**

▼**RECOMMENDED MATERIAL**
Cedar or pine

▼**RECOMMENDED FINISH**
Clear water sealer

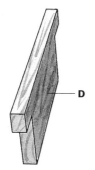

D

FIGURE 1

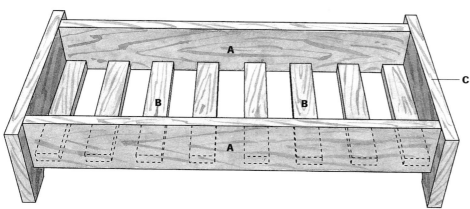

▼**MATERIALS**

(for one 10-inch x 24-inch tray)
$4\frac{1}{2}$ linear feet of 1 x 4 stock
$6\frac{1}{2}$ linear feet of 1 x 2 stock
$3\frac{1}{2}$ linear feet of 1 x 6 stock

(for one 14-inch x 30-inch tray)
$5\frac{1}{2}$ linear feet of 1 x 4 stock
12 linear feet of 1 x 2 stock
5 linear feet of 1 x 6 stock

▼**HARDWARE**

(for one 10-inch x 24-inch tray)
32 4d finishing nails
8   $1\frac{1}{2}$" decking screws

(for one 10-inch x 24-inch tray)
40 4d finishing nails
8   $1\frac{1}{2}$" decking screws

▼**ADDITIONAL TOOLS**
Dinner plate or other round object
Jigsaw or coping saw

INSTRUCTIONS

1. Cut two **side pieces** (A).

2. Cut eight (or ten, if you're building the larger tray) **slats** (B).

3. Lay the **side pieces** (A) on edge, parallel and ends even.

4. Using Figure 1 as a guide, place a **slat** (B) face down between the **side pieces** (A), outside edge flush with the ends of the **side pieces**. Clamp the pieces in place; then nail the **slat** in place with two 4d finishing nails through the face of each **side piece** into the ends of the **slat**.

5. Measure $1\frac{1}{2}$ inches in from the first **slat** (B) and mark this point on the inside faces of the **side pieces** (A). Place a second **slat** with its outside edge at this line and nail it in place as before. Repeat until all eight (or ten, if you're building the larger tray) **slats** are nailed in place. There should be a $1\frac{1}{2}$-inch space between the edges of each **slat**, and the edge of the last **slat** should be flush with the ends of the **side pieces**.

▼**CUTTING LIST**

(for one 10-inch x 24-inch tray)

CODE	DESCRIPTION	QTY.	MATERIAL	DIMENSIONS
A	Sides	2	1 x 4 stock	$22\frac{1}{2}$" long
B	Slats	8	1 x 2 stock	$8\frac{1}{2}$" long
C	End pieces	2	1 x 6 stock	12" long
D	Divider	1	1 x 6 stock	10" long

(for one 10-inch x 24-inch tray)

CODE	DESCRIPTION	QTY.	MATERIAL	DIMENSIONS
A	Sides	2	1 x 4 stock	$28\frac{1}{2}$" long
B	Slats	10	1 x 2 stock	$12\frac{1}{2}$" long
C	End pieces	2	1 x 6 stock	16" long
D	Divider	1	1 x 6 stock	14" long

6. Cut two **end pieces** (C).

7. Take a good look at Figure 2; it shows the shape that the **end pieces** (C) should be cut into. As you can, each **end piece** has a slight arc centered along one edge.

8. To cut the arc on the **end pieces** (C), start by placing the edge of a plate or some other large, round object against one **end piece**, centering the plate on the **end piece's** face, about 1 inch from the **end piece's** edge. Trace around the round object's edge to mark a gentle arc centered on one edge of the **end piece**.

9. Use a jigsaw or a coping saw to cut the arc on the **end piece** (C).

10. To make sure that the **end pieces** (C) have symmetrical curves, place the cut **end piece** on top of the uncut **end piece**, edges and ends even. Trace the arc onto the second **end piece** and cut it out as before.

11. Using Figure 1 as a guide, place an **end piece** (C) at both ends of the side piece and slat assembly, with the flat edges of the **end pieces** flush with the edges of the **side pieces** (A) that are opposite the edges to which the **slats** (B) are attached. Clamp the pieces in place; then screw through the **end pieces** into the ends of the **side pieces**, using two 1½-inch screws at each joint.

12. Cut the **divider** (D).

13. Take a close look at Figure 3; this is the shape that you'll need to cut the **divider** (D) into.

14. To cut the **divider's** (D) shape, start by measuring down 2 inches from one edge of the **divider**; mark a line across the length of the board at this point.

15. Measure in ¾ inch from both ends of the **divider** (D) and mark a line across the width of the board at this point.

16. The lines from steps 14 and 15 will form long rectangles at both ends of the **divider** (D). Cut out these rectangles.

17. Place the **divider** (D) into the seedling tray, fitting its bottom edge between one of the spaces between the **slats** (B).

18. If the **divider** won't fit into the seedling tray, you may need to sand or file the cut portion of the ends of the **divider** until the piece fits properly.

19. Smooth any of the seedling tray's rough edges and ends with sandpaper, and finish as desired.

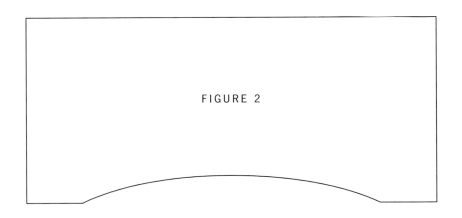

FIGURE 2

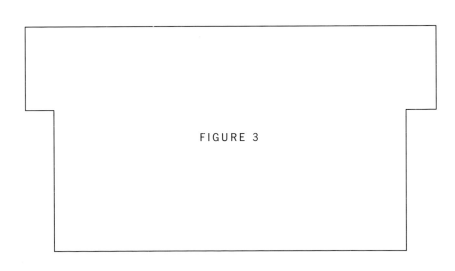

FIGURE 3

BOOT BENCH

The boot bench shown in the photos is made from salvaged barn wood, but because most folks don't have access to abandoned barns, we've modified the directions to make use of standard lumber. Your bench will look slightly different from the one in the photos because you'll be using new lumber in standard dimensions; therefore, we've included a step for giving the bench a "weathered" look. We've also added corner blocks—which you'll see in the illustrations, but not in the photos—and made minor adjustments to several joints for added strength.

▼ CUTTING LIST

CODE	DESCRIPTION	QTY.	MATERIAL	DIMENSIONS
A	Front pieces	2	2 x 8 stock	48" long
B	Back pieces	2	2 x 8 stock	45" long
C	Corner blocks	4	2 x 4 stock	13⅛" long
D	Side pieces	4	2 x 8 stock	17" long
E	Bottom pieces	2	2 x 8 stock	6¹⁵⁄₁₆" x 45" long
F	Feet	2	2 x 8 stock	17" long
G	Wide back verticals	6	2 x 8 stock	48" long
H	Narrow back vertical	1	2 x 4 stock	2¼" x 48"
I	Back support	1	1 x 4 stock	48" long
J	Hinge strip	1	2 x 4 stock	2¾" x 48"
K	Top pieces	2	2 x 8 stock	48" long
L	Top cleats	2	1 x 4 stock	12¾" long

▼ RECOMMENDED MATERIAL
Pressure-treated pine or spruce for the feet (F), and cedar or pine for all other pieces

▼ RECOMMENDED FINISH
Polyurethane finish

▼ MATERIALS
64 linear feet of 2 x 8 stock
14 linear feet of 2 x 4 stock
7 linear feet of 1 x 4 stock
3 linear feet of 2 x 8 PT stock
1 large pad of fine steel wool
1 gallon of apple cider vinegar

▼ HARDWARE
100 2½" decking screws
14 2" decking screws
2 4" x 4" butt hinges and accompanying hardware

▼ ADDITIONAL TOOLS
Circular saw and rip fence
Jigsaw or coping saw
60"-long strip of flexible wood or metal

DESIGNER: **DAVID PENLAND**

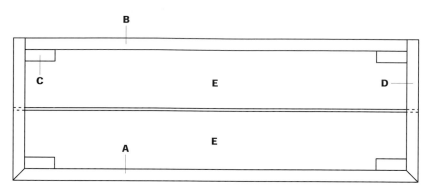

FIGURE 1, top view of bench box assembly

INSTRUCTIONS

1. Cut two **front pieces** (A). As Figures 1 and 2 show, the **front pieces** and the **side pieces** (D) meet in a miter joint at the front corners of the bench, so you must mark and cut a 45° bevel on the inside faces at each end of both **front pieces**. Mark and cut the angles.

2. Cut two **back pieces** (B) and four **corner blocks** (C).

3. On each **corner block** (C), measure $1\frac{1}{2}$ inches in from one edge and mark a line along the length of the piece at this point.

4. On the line that you marked in step 3, measure in from one end (this will be the top end) of each **corner block** (C) and mark the following points: $1\frac{1}{2}$ inches; $5\frac{3}{4}$ inches; $8\frac{7}{8}$ inches; and $12\frac{5}{8}$ inches. Two of the **corner blocks** will be attached at the back of the bench and two will be attached at the front, so you'll need to make the marks in this step as mirror images on the two pairs.

5. Place the **front pieces** (A) on a flat work surface, ends even, with a $\frac{1}{8}$-inch space between their edges. The face of the bevels at each end should face up.

6. Place one **corner block** (C), with the marked face up, across the two **front pieces** (A), with the edge opposite the line from step 3 flush with the inside of the bevel, and the top end flush with the top edge of the upper **front piece**. There should be a $1\frac{1}{2}$-inch space between the bottom end of the **corner block** and the bottom edge of the bottom **front piece**. Clamp the pieces in place. Screw through the **corner block** into the **front pieces** at each of the marks you made in step 4, using $2\frac{1}{2}$-inch screws.

7. Repeat step 6 to attach another **corner block** (C) to the other end of the front-piece assembly. This completes the front assembly.

8. Place the **back pieces** (B) face-down on a flat work surface, with their ends even and a $\frac{1}{8}$-inch space between their edges.

9. Place a **corner block** (C), with the marked face up, across the two **back pieces** (B), with the top end of the **corner block** flush with the top edge of the upper **back piece**, and the edge opposite the marks from step 4 flush with the ends of the **back pieces**. Clamp the pieces in place and attach as before. Repeat on the other side with the remaining **corner block**. This completes the back assembly.

10. Cut four **side pieces** (D). Using Figure 1 as a guide, mark and cut a 45° bevel on the inside face of one end of each **side piece**.

11. Place the front assembly on a flat work surface, on edge, with its bottom edge down. Place one **side piece** (D), on edge, at a right angle to the front assembly with its bottom edge down and the beveled edge flush against the beveled edge of the bottom **front piece** (A). Clamp the pieces in place. Attach them by screwing through the **side piece** into the edge of the adjacent **corner block** (C) on the **front piece**, with two $2\frac{1}{2}$-inch screws.

12. Repeat step 11 to attach a **side piece** (D) to the other side of the front assembly.

13. Using Figure 1 as a guide, place the back assembly inside the **side pieces** (D) that are attached to the front assembly, with the ends of the **back pieces** (B) inside the **side pieces**, and the ends of the **side pieces** flush with the face of the **back pieces**. Clamp the pieces in place. Screw through each **side piece** into the edge of the adjacent **corner block** (C) on each **back piece**, with two $2\frac{1}{2}$-inch screws.

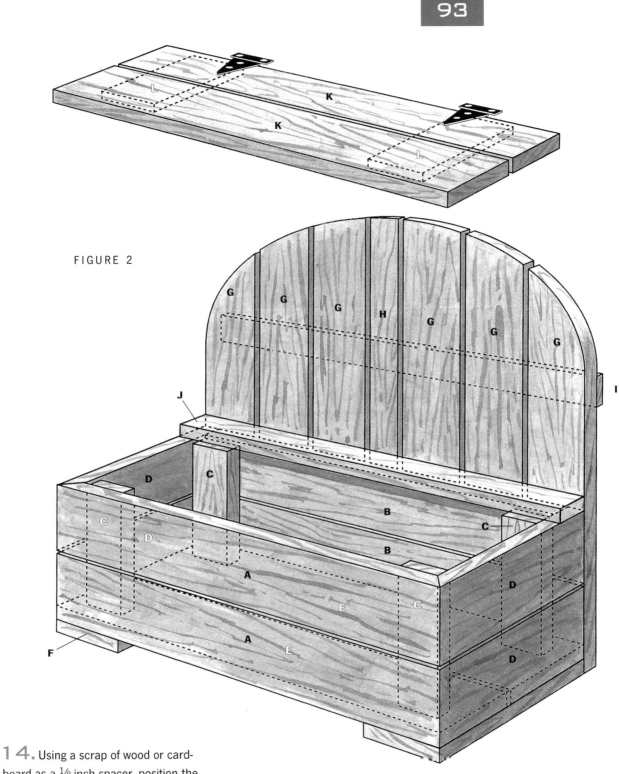

FIGURE 2

14. Using a scrap of wood or cardboard as a ⅛-inch spacer, position the remaining **side pieces** (D) in place between the front and back assemblies and above the bottom **side pieces**. Clamp the pieces in place, and attach them with two 2½-inch screws into each adjacent **corner block** (C).

15. Cut two 45-inch lengths from 2 x 8 stock. Rip a 6¹⁵⁄₁₆-inch-wide **bottom piece** (E) from each length.

16. Place the rectangular frame you completed in step 14 on a flat work sur-

face, top edge down. Place a **bottom piece** (E) inside the rectangular frame, resting on top of the **corner blocks** (C), with one edge butting up against the inside face of the front assembly. Screw through the bottom **front piece** (A) into the edge of the **bottom piece**, with four evenly spaced 2½-inch screws. Then screw through the bottom **side pieces** (D) into the ends of the **bottom piece**, using two 2½-inch screws at each joint.

17. Place the second **bottom piece** (E) inside the frame with one edge butted up against the inside face of the back assembly. Attach the **bottom piece** to the rectangular frame following the technique in step 16.

18. Cut two **feet** (F). Place one **foot** across the **bottom pieces** (E), with one edge flush with the face of the adjoining **side piece** (D), and its ends flush with the faces of the **front** and **back pieces** (A and B). Screw through the **foot** into the **bottom pieces**, using three evenly spaced 2-½-inch screws along each of the **foot's** edges. Attach the second foot to the other side of the box assembly the same way.

19. Cut six **wide back verticals** (G). Then cut a 48-inch length from 2 x 4 stock. Rip the 2¼-inch-wide **narrow back vertical** (H) from this length.

20. On a flat work surface, lay out the **wide back verticals** (G) and the **narrow back vertical** (H), ends even, with a ⅜-inch space between their edges. The **narrow back vertical** should be in the center. From the outside edge of the outermost board on one side to the outside edge of the outermost board on the other side, the **back verticals** together should be 48 inches across. (You may need to adjust the spaces between the boards to get

the 48-inch distance, due to variations in the width of the 2 x 8 lumber.)

21. Designate one end of the **back verticals** (G and H) as the bottom. From this end, measure up 36 inches along the outside edge of the two outermost pieces and mark this point on both boards.

22. Find the center, widthwise, of the **narrow back vertical** (H) and mark this point at the top end of the board.

23. Use a thin, flexible strip of wood or metal to create an arc connecting the 36-inch marks on the outermost **wide back verticals** (G) and the center

mark on the **narrow back vertical** (H). Mark this arc across the face of the **back verticals**.

24. Use a jigsaw or a saber saw to cut the arc on the **back verticals** (G and H).

25. Using Figure 2 as a guide, place one of the outermost **wide back verticals** (G) against the **back pieces** (B) on the box, with its outside edge flush with the face of the adjoining **side piece** (D) and its bottom end flush with the bottom edge of the **back piece**. Clamp the pieces in place. Screw through the **wide back vertical** into the adjoining **back pieces** with three evenly spaced 2½-inch screws along both of the **wide back vertical's** edges.

26. Using Figure 2 as a guide, attach the remaining **back verticals** (G and H), leaving a space of approximately ³⁄₈ inch between each one, and following the same technique used in step 25. Note that the center **narrow back vertical** (H) requires only three screws.

27. On the back face of the outermost **wide back verticals** (G), measure 35 inches up from the bottom end and mark this point.

28. Cut the **back support** (I). Position it across the **back verticals** (G and H) with its top edge even with the marks from step 27 and its ends flush with the edges of the outermost **wide back verticals**. Clamp the pieces in place. Screw through the **back support** into the adjoining **back verticals**, using two 2¹⁄₂-inch screws at each **wide back vertical**, and one 2¹⁄₂-inch screw at the **narrow back vertical**.

29. Cut a 48-inch length from 2 x 4 stock. Rip the 2-inch-wide **hinge strip** (J) from this length.

30. Position the **hinge strip** (J) with one 1¹⁄₂-inch edge against the **back verticals** (G and H), and on top of the back edge of the back assembly. The ends should be flush with the faces of the **side pieces** (D) and the **hinge strip's** 2-inch face should be up. Clamp the pieces in place. Screw through the **hinge strip** into the upper edge of the top **back piece** (B), using eight evenly spaced 2¹⁄₂-inch screws.

31. Cut two **top pieces** (K) and two **top cleats** (L).

32. Place the **top pieces** (K) face-down on a flat work surface with their ends even and a ¹⁄₈-inch space between their edges. Measure in 6 inches from each end of the both **top pieces** and mark a line across each piece at these points.

33. Place one **top cleat** (L) face-down across the **top pieces** (K), with one edge on the lines at one end of the **top pieces**, and one end ¹⁄₄ inch in from one edge of one **top piece**. Clamp the pieces in place. Screw through the **top cleat** into the **top pieces**, using two 2-inch screws into each **top piece**.

34. Repeat step 33 at the other end of the **top pieces** (K) with the remaining **top cleat** (L).

35. Position the top assembly on the bench box; the edge with the ¹⁄₄-inch space to the **top cleats** should be toward the **hinge strip** (J), leaving a ¹⁄₄-inch gap between the top assembly and the edge of the **hinge strip**. The ends of the top should be flush with the faces of the sides. The front edge of the top should extend beyond the front of the bench box by about ³⁄₄ inch.

36. Position one hinge on the **hinge strip** (J) and the top assembly, 6 inches in from one end of the top assembly. Center the pin of the hinge over the gap between the top assembly and the hinge strip. Fasten the hinge to both pieces using the hardware provided.

37. Position and fasten the remaining hinge to the **hinge strip** (J) and the top assembly at the other side of the bench box, following the techniques in step 36.

38. Fill all the screw holes in the exposed pieces. Sand all the pieces smooth, slightly rounding the edges and corners of the bench.

39. To give your bench a "weathered finish," start by putting a large pad of fine steel wool into a gallon of apple cider vinegar. Let the vinegar stand for one week, or until the steel wool dissolves completely. The liquid will have thickened slightly. Stir it well, then paint it onto all the surfaces of the bench. Let the bench dry well. Then wipe off any residue with a soft cloth and apply a polyurethane finish.

HANGING WINE CHILLER

Just because you're entertaining outdoors doesn't mean you have to choose between hiding a dingy plastic ice chest and sipping lukewarm chardonnay. Simply fill this unusual wine chiller with crushed ice and a bottle of your favorite beverage; then hang it from the nearest tree branch or a corner of your picnic table. Its loose, yet sturdy construction will allow water from melting ice to drain easily, and its good looks will enhance any outdoor gathering.

▼ **RECOMMENDED MATERIAL**

(A, A) or (A, B) birch or cedar lumber-core exterior-grade plywood

▼ **RECOMMENDED FINISH**

Exterior stain

▼ **MATERIALS AND SUPPLIES**

1 piece of ½-inch exterior-grade
   plywood, 4' x 4'

3 pieces of ¼-inch white nylon cord,
   each 5' long

▼ **ADDITIONAL TOOLS**

Jigsaw or coping saw

Router with roundover bit (optional)

Matches or a lighter (to "solder" the
   ends of the nylon cord)

▼ **CUTTING LIST**

CODE	DESCRIPTION	QTY.	MATERIAL	DIMENSIONS
A	Side pieces	12	½" plywood	As shown in Figure 1
B	Base	1	½" plywood	6¼"-diameter circle

INSTRUCTIONS

1. Make a copy of Figure 1 and use a photocopier to enlarge it until it is 3 inches across at its wide end and 2 inches across at its narrow end. This is the pattern for cutting the wine chiller's **side pieces** (A).

2. Transfer the **side piece** (A) pattern to the plywood twelve times and cut out the pieces with a jigsaw or a coping saw.

3. At both ends of each **side piece** (A), bore two ⅜-inch holes, locating them ½ inch in from each edge and ½ inch from each end.

4. Use a compass to trace a 6¼-inch-diameter circle onto the exterior-grade plywood. This will be the wine chiller's **base** (B). Cut out the **base** with a jigsaw or coping saw.

5. Bore eleven ⅜-inch holes through the **base** (B), locating them ½ inch in from the circumference and 1½ inches apart.

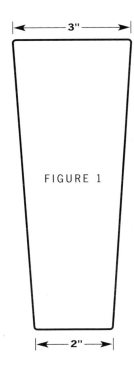

FIGURE 1

3"

2"

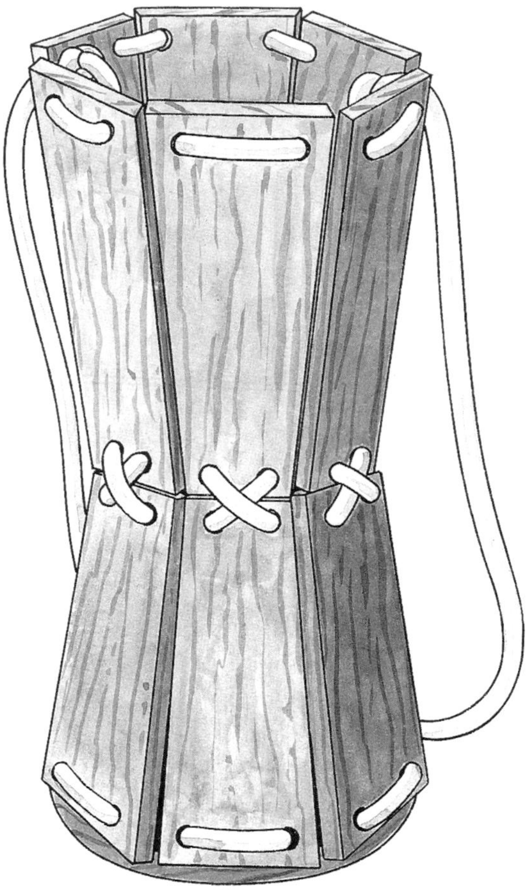

FIGURE 2

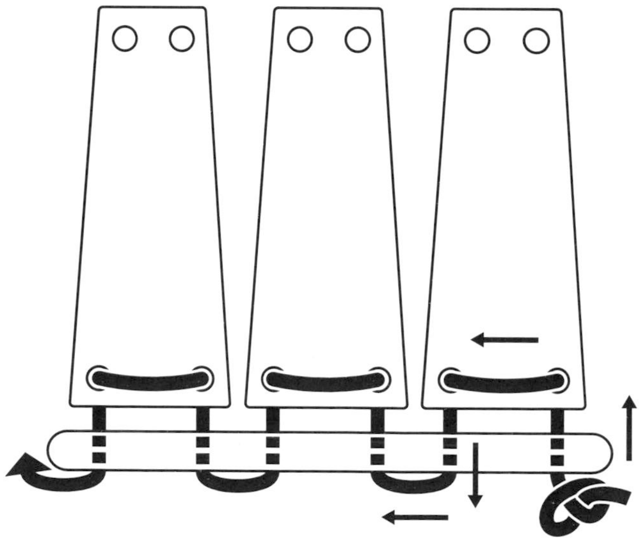

FIGURE 3

6. Smooth the edges of all the pieces with a rasp, file, and sandpaper, or a router and a roundover bit.

7. Finish all the pieces with an exterior stain and let them dry completely.

8. To assemble the wine chiller, start by taking a good look at Figure 2 to see how the **side pieces** (A) are oriented. There are six **side pieces** in each of the two tiers that form the body of the project.

9. To attach the first tier of six **side pieces** (A) to the **base** (B), start by tying a knot at one end of one piece of the cord. "Solder" the knot with a match or a lighter; this will keep the nylon from unraveling.

10. Referring to Figure 3, weave the cord up and through the base. Then weave it from the right to the left of the wide end of a **side piece** (A) and back down through the **base** (B).

11. Continue to weave around the **base** (B) until you've attached six **side pieces** (A). Tie a knot on the inside of the tier and solder it with a match. Trim the excess rope.

12. To attach the second tier of **side pieces** (A) to the first tier of **side pieces**, start by tying a knot at one end of a second piece of nylon cord. Solder the knot with a match.

13. Take a good look at Figure 4, which shows how to run the cord to attach the bottom tier of **side pieces** (A) to the top tier. You'll weave the rope from the back to the front of the right hole in the narrow end of one of the bottom **side pieces**, through the front of the left hole in the narrow end of the top **side piece**. Thread the cord through the back of the right hole in the top **side piece**, around to the front of the left hole in the bottom **side piece**. Continue this "stitch" to attach all six of the top tier **side pieces**. Tie a knot on the inside of the tiers, solder it with a match, and trim the excess rope.

14. Tie and solder a knot at one end of the last piece of nylon cord. Use it to weave together the top of the second tier **side pieces** (A), using Figure 5 as a guide. You'll simply run the cord through all the holes at the top (wide) end of the **side pieces**.

15. Use Figure 6 as a guide to form the loop for suspending the wine chiller. You'll loop the free end of the rope around part of itself anywhere at the top of the wine chiller; then loop the rope around itself at a point directly opposite before tying and soldering a knot in the free end. Trim the excess rope.

16. To use, fill the bottom with about four inches of crushed ice. Place a bottle of wine inside, and fill the rest of the wine chiller with more crushed ice.

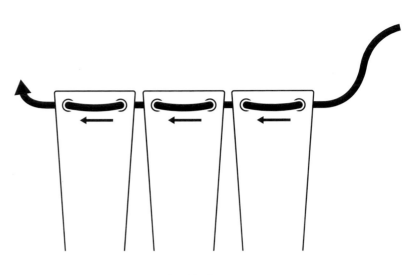

FIGURE 5

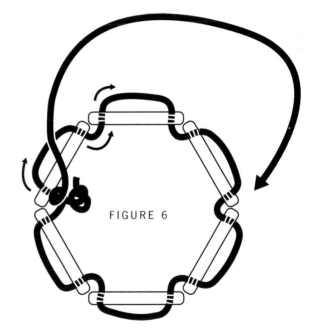

FIGURE 6

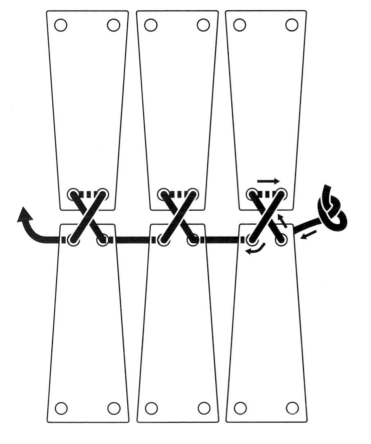

FIGURE 4

CANDLEHOLDERS

The sun begins to set and the summer night settles in. Why not complete the scene with candlelight? Nothing could be easier than creating your own wooden candleholders, just right for outdoor dining. Leave them simple, or embellish them with strips of metal, bits of tile, or lengths of wooden dowel. The directions below will yield two 3½-inch-high candleholders, which is the size of the shortest candleholder shown in the project photo. To make candleholders in other sizes, simply cut the 4 x 4 stock to the desired length—all of the other dimensions remain the same.

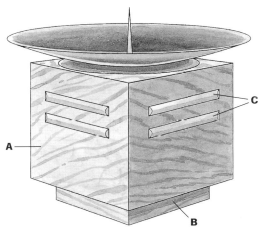

▼ CUTTING LIST

CODE	DESCRIPTION	QTY.	MATERIAL	DIMENSIONS
A	Body	2	4 x 4 stock	2½" long
B	Base	2	1 x 3 stock	2½" long
C	Dowel pieces	8	¼" dowel	3" long

▼ RECOMMENDED MATERIAL
Cedar or pine

▼ RECOMMENDED FINISH
Exterior stain

▼ MATERIALS AND SUPPLIES
(for two 3½-inch-high candleholders)

½ linear foot of 4 x 4 stock

½ linear foot of 1 x 3 stock

4 linear feet of ¼" dowel (optional)

16–24 pieces brass sheet, each
   ½" x 2½" (optional)

2 metal candle dishes, 5⅜" in
   diameter with center spikes (The
   center spikes are optional.)

Exterior wood glue

High-strength epoxy (Look for a brand
   that will hold metal and wood.)

▼ HARDWARE
8   3d finishing nails

▼ ADDITIONAL TOOL
Tin snips (if using brass sheet to decorate candleholders)

INSTRUCTIONS

1. Cut two **bodies** (A) and two **bases** (B). Lightly sand both pieces, but leave the corners square. Finish the **body** and **base** pieces with the stain or paint of your choice, and allow the finish to dry.

2. Using the illustration as a guide, center a **base** (B) over one end of one **body** (A). Secure the pieces with four 3d finishing nails. Repeat with the remaining **body** and **base**.

3. If you're using dowel pieces to decorate your candleholder, clamp the dowel to a bench top or other flat work surface. Use a wood file to flatten the dowel so that the remaining wood is semicircular in profile. Cut the dowel into sixteen **dowel pieces** (C).

4. Using the illustration as a guide, bevel both ends of each **dowel piece** (C) to roughly 45°.

5. On each body-base assembly, measure points ⅜ inch and 1⅛ inches down from the top end of the **body** (A); square a line around all four sides of the **body** at these points.

6. Glue a **dowel piece** (C) (or, if you prefer, a piece of brass sheet) under each mark that you made in step 5, being careful to center the **dowel pieces** across the width of the **body** (A); there should be about ¼ inch between the end of each **dowel piece** and the edge of the body.

7. Use high-strength epoxy to glue a candle dish to the top of each **body** (A).

DESIGNER: **MARK STROM**

DUCKBOARD BENCH

Based on the same simple design as the duckboard square (page 68) and the duckboard table (page 105), this attractive bench is almost as easy to build as it is to enjoy. Finish it with a clear sealer for a natural look (as shown), or paint it an eye-catching color to accent any part of your garden, backyard, or porch.

▼CUTTING LIST

CODE	DESCRIPTION	QTY.	MATERIAL	DIMENSIONS
A	Long sides	2	1 x 2 stock	34" long
B	Short sides	2	1 x 2 stock	15" long
C	Top brace	1	1 x 2 stock	32½" long
D	Slats	14	1 x 2 stock	16½" long
E	Leg pieces	8	1 x 3 stock	15" long
F	Short leg braces	2	1 x 2 stock	13½" long
G	Long leg braces	2	1 x 2 stock	29½" long

▼RECOMMENDED MATERIAL
Cypress or pressure-treated pine or spruce

▼RECOMMENDED FINISH
Clear water sealer or exterior paint

▼MATERIALS AND SUPPLIES
40 linear feet of 1 x 2 stock
12 linear feet of 1 x 3 stock
Exterior wood glue

▼HARDWARE
22 1⅝" decking screws
62 1¼" decking screws

▼ADDITIONAL TOOL
Router with a ¼" roundover bit
   (optional)

INSTRUCTIONS

1. Cut two **long sides** (A) and two **short sides** (B).

2. On a flat surface, using the illustration on the next page as a guide, form a rectangle by placing the **short sides** (B) between the **long sides** (A), making sure that the ends of the **long sides** are flush with the outside faces of the **short sides**. Screw through the **long sides** into the ends of the **short sides**, using one 1⅝-inch screw at each joint.

3. Cut the **top brace** (C), checking its length against the inside of the rectangle before cutting.

DESIGNER: **ROBIN CLARK**

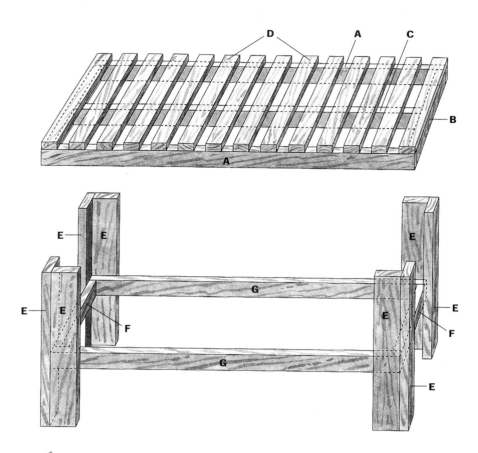

1 1. Fit a leg assembly into one corner of the rectangular bench top. The wide face of the leg assembly should be against a **long side** (A). Screw through each **leg piece** (E) into the adjoining **long** or **short side** (A or B), using one 1¼-inch screw at each joint.

1 2. Repeat step 11 to attach the other three leg assemblies.

1 3. Cut two **short leg braces** (F). Before making the cut, check the pieces against the legs near the bench seat and allow for the thickness of the **long leg braces** (G).

1 4. Cut two **long leg braces** (G), checking the pieces against the legs near the seat before cutting.

4. Center the **top brace** (C), on edge, inside the rectangle assembly. Screw through the **short sides** (B) into the ends of the **top brace**, using one 1⅝-inch screw at each joint.

5. Cut fourteen **slats** (D). Use a rasp and file or a router with a roundover bit to round over the **slats'** edges.

6. Using the illustration as a guide, lay the **slats** (D) facedown across the rectangle. You may space all fourteen **slats** evenly, or you may place two together at the center of the rectangle, with the remaining **slats** spaced evenly, as shown in the project photo.

7. Screw through the **slats** (D) into the adjacent edges of the **long sides** (A), using one 1⅝-inch screw at each joint.

joint. Then screw through the twelve center **slats** into the edge of the **top brace** (C), using one 1-5/8-inch screw at each joint.

8. Cut eight **leg pieces** (E).

9. To assemble a leg, place one **leg piece** (E) against another, as shown in the illustration. The edge of one **leg piece** should be flush with the face of the other and their ends should be even. Glue the pieces and clamp them together while the glue cures. Then screw through the face of one **leg piece** into the edge of the other **leg piece**, using four evenly spaced 1⅝-inch screws.

1 0. Repeat step 9 three times to make three more leg assemblies.

1 5. Using the illustration as a guide, position a **long leg brace** (G) between two leg assemblies, 5½ inches up from the legs' bottom ends. Screw through the **long leg brace** into the faces of the adjoining **leg pieces** (E), using one 1¼-inch screw at each joint. Attach the other **long leg brace** opposite from the first.

1 6. Position a **short leg brace** (F) between two of the **long leg braces** (G), as shown in the illustration. Screw through the **short leg brace** into the adjoining **leg pieces** (E), using one 1¼-inch screw at each joint. Attach the other **short leg brace** opposite from the first.

1 7. Use a rasp and file or a router with a roundover bit to round over all exposed edges. Finish with sandpaper and the stain or paint of your choice.

DUCKBOARD TABLE

Just as you settle in for a relaxing afternoon read, you realize you have no place to set your iced tea and sunglasses. Far better looking than anything you'll find in garden stores, this easy-to-make table will hold all your outdoor-relaxation essentials in style. Start work on it in the morning, and you'll have plenty of time left to enjoy it the same afternoon.

▼**RECOMMENDED MATERIAL**
Cypress or pressure-treated pine or spruce

▼**RECOMMENDED FINISH**
Clear water sealer or exterior paint

▼**MATERIALS AND SUPPLIES**
20 linear feet of 1 x 2 stock
12 linear feet of 1 x 3 stock
Exterior wood glue

▼**HARDWARE**
20 $1\frac{5}{8}$" decking screws
34 $1\frac{1}{4}$" decking screws

▼**ADDITIONAL TOOL**
Router with a $\frac{1}{4}$" roundover bit (optional)

▼**CUTTING LIST**

CODE	DESCRIPTION	QTY.	MATERIAL	DIMENSIONS
A	Long sides	2	1 x 2 stock	$16\frac{1}{2}$" long
B	Short sides	2	1 x 2 stock	15" long
C	Slats	7	1 x 2 stock	$16\frac{1}{2}$" long
D	Leg pieces	8	1 x 3 stock	$16\frac{1}{2}$" long
E	Long braces	2	1 x 2 stock	$13\frac{1}{2}$" long
F	Short braces	2	1 x 2 stock	12" long

INSTRUCTIONS

1. To make the tabletop, cut the **long sides** (A) and the **short sides** (B). Then follow the directions for building a duckboard square on page 69.

2. Cut eight **leg pieces** (D).

3. To assemble a leg, place one **leg piece** (D) against another, as shown in the illustration on the following page. The edge of one leg piece should be flush with the face of the other and their ends should be even. Glue the pieces and clamp them together while the glue cures. Then screw through the face of one **leg piece** into the edge of the other **leg piece**, using four evenly spaced $1\frac{5}{8}$-inch screws.

4. Repeat step 3 three times to make the other leg assemblies.

5. Fit a leg assembly into one corner of the tabletop. Screw through the **leg pieces** (D) into the adjacent **long** and **short sides** (A and B), using one $1\frac{1}{4}$-inch screw at each joint.

6. Repeat step 5 to attach the remaining leg assemblies in the other corners of the tabletop.

7. Cut two **long braces** (E), checking the pieces against the legs near the table top before making the cut.

8. Cut two **short braces** (F). Before making the cut, check the pieces against the legs near the tabletop and allow for the thickness of the long leg braces.

9. Using the illustration as a guide, position a **long brace** (E) between two legs, about 5½ inches up from the legs' bottom ends. Screw through the **long brace** into the faces of the adjoining **leg pieces** (D), using one 1¼-inch screw at each joint. Attach the other **long brace** opposite from the first.

10. Position a **short brace** (F) between two of the **long braces** (E). Screw through the **short brace** into the adjoining **leg pieces** (D), using one 1¼-inch screw at each joint.

11. Use a rasp and file or a router with a roundover bit to round over all exposed edges.

12. Smooth with sandpaper and finish with at least two coats of clear water sealer or exterior paint.

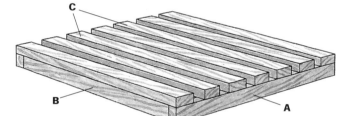

DESIGNER: **ROBIN CLARK**

PICNIC TABLE AND BENCH COMBINATION

Stronger, more durable, and far more attractive than its mass-produced counterparts, this unique picnic table and bench combination will accommodate six diners in comfortable style. It's easy to make, too. Threaded steel rods, two through each side assembly, and another through each connecting brace, hold together standard 2 x 4 lumber cut to length.

▼ CUTTING LIST

CODE	DESCRIPTION	QTY.	MATERIAL	DIMENSIONS
A	Tabletop slats	10	2 x 4 stock	84" long
B	Bench-seat slats	6	2 x 4 stock	84" long
C	Connecting brace pieces	4	2 x 4 stock	61" long
D	Tabletop braces	3	2 x 4 stock	$37\frac{1}{4}$" long
E	Bench-seat braces	4	2 x 4 stock	11" long
F	57" side-assembly pieces	2	2 x 4 stock	57" long
G	45" side-assembly pieces	4	2 x 4 stock	45" long
H	36" side-assembly pieces	4	2 x 4 stock	36" long
I	27" side-assembly pieces	8	2 x 4 stock	27" long
J	18" side-assembly pieces	6	2 x 4 stock	18" long
K	12" side-assembly pieces	4	2 x 4 stock	12" long
L	9" side-assembly pieces	6	2 x 4 stock	9" long
M	Feet	4	2 x 4 stock	6" long
N	$7\frac{1}{2}$" bench pieces	4	2 x 4 stock	$7\frac{1}{2}$" long
O	Bolt covers	4	2 x 4 stock	$3\frac{1}{2}$" x $3\frac{1}{2}$"

DESIGNER: **RALPH SHMITT**

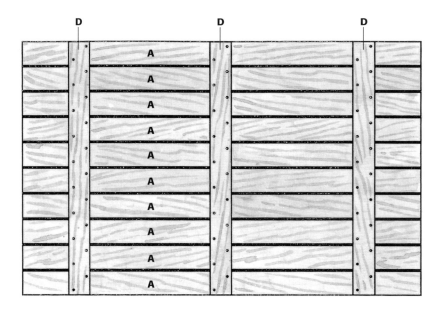

FIGURE 1

▼RECOMMENDED MATERIAL

Cedar or pine

▼RECOMMENDED FINISH

Natural seal with linseed oil

▼MATERIALS

240 linear feet of 2 x 4 stock
(Purchase this in twenty 2 x 4 x 12'
pieces.)

▼HARDWARE

156 $2\frac{1}{2}$" decking screws
2   10' lengths of $\frac{1}{2}$-inch-diameter
     threaded rod
8    $\frac{1}{2}$" x 3" lag screws
20   $\frac{1}{2}$" washers
12   $\frac{1}{2}$" hex nuts
12   $\frac{1}{2}$" lock washers

▼ADDITIONAL TOOLS

Router with fence and $\frac{5}{8}$" straight bit,
   or circular saw and $\frac{1}{2}$" chisel
Hacksaw
Socket wrench for $\frac{1}{2}$" hex nuts
Help from at least one friend

INSTRUCTIONS

1. Because this project consists of so many pieces of varying lengths, it's an exception to the "don't cut until you have to" rule. Start by laying out and measuring all the pieces on the 12-foot 2 x 4 stock, cutting the longest pieces from the straightest stock. Apply the finish of your choice to the pieces; then label them so you'll know what's what.

TABLETOP
(refer to Figure 1)

2. On a large, flat work surface, lay out the ten **tabletop slats** (A), edge to edge with their ends even.

3. From both ends of each **tabletop slat** (A), measure in 8 inches and mark a line across the face of each board at this point.

4. Measure in $40\frac{1}{4}$ inches from both ends of each **tabletop slat** (A) and mark across the face of each board at this point; this will give you two lines, $3\frac{1}{2}$ inches apart, at the center of each board.

5. Arrange the **tabletop slats** (A) so that their edges are $\frac{1}{4}$ inch apart; their ends should still be even. From the outside edge of the outermost board on one side to the outside edge of the outermost board on the other side, the **tabletop slats** should be $37\frac{1}{4}$ inches across.

6. Using Figure 1 as a guide, place a **tabletop brace** (D) facedown across the **tabletop slats** (A), with its outer edge at one of the 8-inch lines you marked in step 3. Place another **tabletop brace** across the **tabletop slats** with its outer edge at the other 8-inch line from step 3. Place the third **tabletop brace** between the lines you marked in step 4. Clamp the pieces in place.

7. Screw through the **tabletop braces** (D) into the adjoining **tabletop slats** (A), using two $2\frac{1}{2}$-inch screws at each **tabletop slat**. (Figure 1 shows where to place the screws.)

BENCH SEATS

8. On a large, flat surface, lay out three of the **bench-seat slats** (B), facedown and edge to edge with their ends even.

9. Repeat steps 3 and 4 on the **bench-seat slats** (B) to mark them for placing the **bench-seat braces** (E).

10. Arrange the **bench-seat slats** (B) so that their edges are ¼ inch apart; their ends should still be even. From the outside edge of the outermost board on one side to the outside edge of the outermost board on the other side, the **bench-seat slats** together should be 11 inches across.

11. Following the same procedure you used in step 6, place the **bench-seat braces** (E) face down across the **bench-seat slats** (B) inside the lines that you marked in step 9.

12. Screw through the **bench-seat braces** (E) into the adjoining **bench-seat slats** (B), using two 2½-inch screws at each **bench-seat slat**.

13. Repeat steps 8–12 to build the second bench seat.

SIDE ASSEMBLIES

(refer to Figure 2)

14. Lay out all of the **side-assembly pieces** (F–L), faceup.

15. Measuring lengthwise, find the center of each **side-assembly piece** (F–L). Square a line across the face of each board at this point.

16. From both sides of the center line that you marked in step 15, measure out 3 inches and square a line across the face of each board at these points.

17. Find the center, widthwise, on each board and mark this point on the lines you made in step 16. You'll use these points to bore holes to accommodate the threaded rods that hold the side assembly together.

18. On two of the **27-inch side-assembly pieces** (I) and two of the **45-inch side-assembly pieces** (G), use a drill with a 1½-inch spade bit to bore a ¾-inch-deep countersink hole at the points from step 17. The **27-inch side-assembly pieces** will be the top boards in each side assembly and the **45-inch side-assembly pieces** will be the bottom boards in each side assembly (see Figure 2). The countersink holes will accommodate the washers and nuts that will secure the threaded rods when you've completed the side assemblies.

19. On the **27-inch side-assembly pieces** (I) from step 18 and on the **57-inch side-assembly pieces** (F), measure in 2 inches from each end and bore ½-inch holes through each board, centered widthwise, for the lag screws that will hold the tabletop to the **27-inch side-assembly pieces** (step 33), and the bench seats to the **57-inch side-assembly pieces** (step 37).

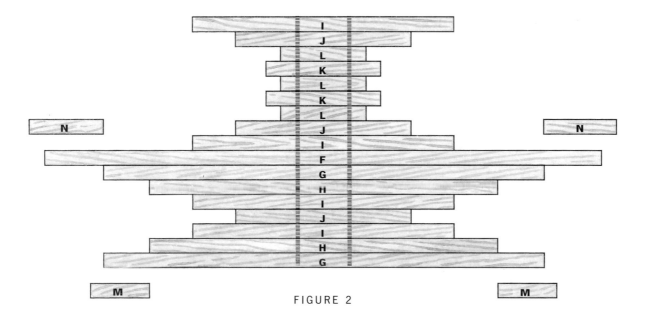

FIGURE 2

FIGURE 3

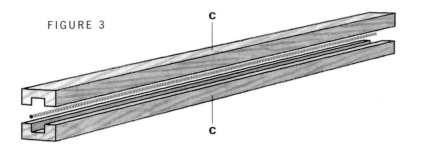

C

C

20. Use a drill with a ⅝-inch spade bit to bore a hole through the face of each side-assembly piece, including the pieces from step 19, centered over the lines 3 inches out from the lengthwise center line.

21. Use a hacksaw to cut two 25¾ inch pieces from both 10-foot lengths of threaded rod. The remaining rods will be about 68½ inches long and you'll use them in step 27 in the **connecting brace pieces** (C).

22. Using Figure 2 as a guide, make two side assemblies. Note that each side assembly is held together by two of the 25¾-inch lengths of threaded rod that fit into the holes from step 20. Start with a **45-inch side-assembly piece** (G) with the 1½-inch countersink holes down, and end with a **27-inch side-assembly piece** (I) with the 1½-inch countersink holes up.

23. Secure the threaded rods with a ½-inch lock washer and a ½-inch nut tightened into the countersink holes on the top **27-inch side-assembly piece** and on the bottom **45-inch side-assembly piece**. If the threaded rod is too long, make sure it protrudes on the bottom end.

24. Using Figure 2 as a guide, clamp a **foot** (M) in place at each end of the bottom **45-inch side-assembly piece** (G) on each side assembly. Screw through each **foot** into the **45-inch side-assembly piece**, with four 2½-inch screws per **foot**.

CONNECTING BRACES
(refer to Figure 3)

25. With a router equipped with a fence and a ⅝-inch straight bit set ⁵⁄₁₆-inch deep, cut a groove centered width-wise along the entire length of the face of each **connecting brace piece** (C). If you don't have a router with a fence and a ⅝-inch cutter, you can use a fence on a circular saw to cut a series of kerfs ⁵⁄₁₆-inch deep along the length of the pieces; then clean out the waste with a ½-inch chisel.

26. Place one **connecting brace piece** (C) over another, grooved face to grooved face, with ends and edges flush. Screw through one **connecting brace piece** into the other, using ten evenly spaced 2½-inch screws along each edge. Repeat with the remaining **connecting brace pieces**.

27. Run a 68½-inch length of threaded rod through the groove in each of the connecting-brace assemblies.

ASSEMBLING THE TABLE
(refer to Figure 4)

28. On both side assemblies, bore a centered ½-inch hole through the edge of the middle **9-inch side-assembly piece** (L) and the bottom **18-inch side-assembly piece** (J).

29. Position one connecting brace between the side assemblies, inserting the ends of the threaded rod of one connecting brace into the ½-inch holes in the **9-inch side-assembly pieces** (L), and the ends of the other connecting brace into the ½-inch holes in the **18-inch side-assembly pieces** (J).

30. Secure both ends of both threaded rods with a ½-inch lock washer and a ½-inch hex nut.

31. Grab a friend to help turn the tabletop over so that the **tabletop slats** (A) are against the ground.

32. From each end of the two outside **tabletop braces** (D), measure in 7⅛ inches and bore a centered ⅜-inch pilot hole, 1 inch deep.

33. Place the tabletop over the side assemblies, brace side down. Attach the pieces with a 3-inch lag screw, a lock washer, and a nut through the holes you bored in step 19, into the ⅜-inch pilot holes that you drilled in the **tabletop braces** (D) in step 32.

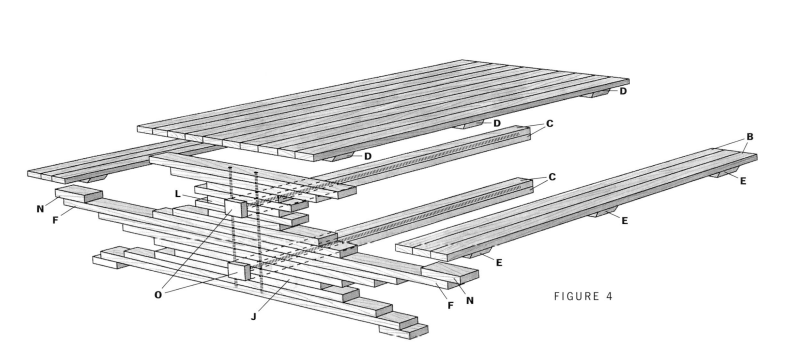

FIGURE 4

34. Turn both bench seats over so that the **bench-seat braces** (E) are facing up.

35. Place a **7¹⁄₂-inch bench piece** (N) on each of the outside **bench-seat braces** (E), edges even and centered lengthwise. Screw through the **7¹⁄₂-inch bench pieces** into the adjoining **bench seat braces**, using four 2¹⁄₂-inch screws on each 7¹⁄₂-inch bench piece (one at each corner).

36. Bore a 1-inch deep, ³⁄₈-inch pilot hole through the center of each 7¹⁄₂-inch bench piece (N). These holes will accommodate the lag screws that will attach the bench-seat assemblies to the side assemblies.

37. Place a bench-seat assembly, brace side down, on top of the **57-inch side-assembly pieces** (F), matching the edges and lining up the pilot holes from steps 19 and 36. Attach the pieces by driving 3-inch lag screws, with washers, through the holes you drilled in step 19 in both ends of both **57-inch side-assembly pieces** and into the ³⁄₈-inch pilot holes you bored in step 36 in the **7¹⁄₂-inch bench pieces** (N).

38. Use a rasp and file to slightly bevel both edges and both ends of one face of each **bolt cover** (O).

39. On the unbeveled face of each **bolt cover** (O), mark the center and use a 1¹⁄₂-inch spade bit to bore a ¹⁄₄-inch-deep countersink hole at this point. Change to a ³⁄₄-inch spade bit, and bore a 1-inch-deep countersink hole, centered in the 1¹⁄₂-inch hole.

40. Glue a **bolt cover** (O) over the ends of the threaded rods, washers, and nuts on the side assemblies (see Figure 4). This completes your picnic table and bench combination.

PORTABLE SUNSHADE

Inspired by Japanese Shoji screens, this stunning project will keep the sun off your shoulders all summer long. When winter weather threatens, bring the sunshade indoors where it will do double duty as an attractive privacy screen or room divider. Although it's designed for use on a porch or other solid surface, adding metal tent stakes to the bottom ends will make it topple-proof for lawn or garden use.

▼ CUTTING LIST

CODE	DESCRIPTION	QTY.	MATERIAL	DIMENSIONS
A	Verticals	12	2 x 2 stock	72" long
B	Horizontals	6	2 x 2 stock	24" long
C	Dowels	6	$5/16$"-diameter dowel	24"-long

▼ RECOMMENDED MATERIAL
Cedar or pine

▼ RECOMMENDED FINISH
Clear, water-based exterior wood finish

▼ MATERIALS AND SUPPLIES
112 linear feet of 2 x 2 stock (Purchase this in fourteen 2 x 2 x 8' pieces.)

4 pieces of preshrunk canvas fabric, each 17" x 69"

12 linear feet of $5/16$"-diameter wooden dowel

▼ HARDWARE
24   $1\frac{1}{4}$" decking screws

4   $3\frac{1}{2}$" x $3\frac{1}{2}$" square butt hinges and accompanying hardware

12   metal tent stakes (optional)

▼ ADDITIONAL TOOLS
Backsaw and miter box

Router and $\frac{1}{2}$" straight bit (optional)

Sewing machine or a friend who knows how to sew

NOTE: *Each of the three panels for this sunshade requires four **verticals** (A) and two **horizontals** (B). The pieces are joined with carefully measured and cut half-lap joints. Make one panel at a time, and measure the marked half-lap joints against the actual pieces to ensure an exact fit.*

DESIGNER: **JOE ARCHIBALD**

INSTRUCTIONS

1. Cut twelve **verticals** (A) and six **horizontals** (B).

2. On a large, flat work surface, lay out four **verticals** (A), edge to edge and ends even. Clamp the pieces in place.

3. From both ends of each of the four **verticals** (A), measure in and square lines across the pieces at $1\frac{1}{2}$ inches and 3 inches. These sets of lines at both ends of the **verticals** will show you where to cut the dadoes for the half-lap joints that join the **horizontals** (B). Select and label the **horizontal** that will fit into each joint, label the joint, and check the marks against the actual **horizontal**; adjust the marks as necessary.

4. To mark the points where you'll bore holes for the **dowels** (C), start by measuring in 4 inches from each end of each of the four **verticals** (A); square a line across the four **verticals** at this point.

5. Unclamp the **verticals** (A).

6. Square the lines that you marked in step 3 around the adjoining edges on each **vertical** (A). On each edge, find the center, widthwise, and mark a straight line at this point between the lines you just squared. This line marks the depth to cut to when making the dadoes for the half-lap joints.

7. Square the lines that you marked in step 4 around the adjoining edges of each **vertical** (A); then find the center of each piece, widthwise, and mark this point across the 4-inch lines; this marks where you'll bore the holes for the **dowels** (C).

8. On a large, flat work surface, lay out the two **horizontals** (B) from step 3, edge to edge and ends even. Clamp the pieces in place.

9. From both ends of each **horizontal** (B), measure in and square lines across the pieces at $1\frac{1}{2}$ inches, $2\frac{1}{2}$ inches, and 4 inches. The space between the end of each **horizontal** and the $1\frac{1}{2}$-inch line shows where to cut the first dado and the space between the $2\frac{1}{2}$-inch line and 4-inch line shows where to cut the second one. Using the labels from step 3, check the marks against the **vertical** (A) that will fit into each joint; make adjustments as necessary.

10. Unclamp the **horizontals** (B).

11. Repeat the technique described in step 6 to mark the depth of the dadoes for the half-lap joints on the **horizontals** (B).

12. Using the illustrations on page 27 as a guide, cut the dadoes that you marked on each piece. Start by using a backsaw and a miter box to make a cut at each line representing the end of the dado; then make a series of cuts, approximately $\frac{1}{8}$ inch apart, between these two lines. Use a sharp chisel to clean out the remaining wood, making sure that the bottom of the dado is flat. (If you have one, a router with a $\frac{1}{2}$-inch straight bit will make removing the waste easier. Make sure you cut the shoulders of the dado first, then step down to the $\frac{3}{4}$-inch depth, routing $\frac{1}{4}$ inch deep first, then $\frac{1}{2}$ inch, and finally $\frac{3}{4}$ inch.)

13. Using the illustration as a guide, join the pieces together to test the fit of the joints. They should be snug, but not too tight; a few taps with a hammer should be enough to secure the joint. If the fit is too tight, adjust it by removing a little more wood from the inside of the dado, using a sharp chisel.

14. Disassemble the pieces.

15. On one edge of the two **verticals** (A) that will be on the outside of the panel, bore a $\frac{3}{4}$-inch-diameter hole, $\frac{1}{2}$ inch deep at each of the points you marked in step 7. This will be the outside-facing edge on these two **verticals**. Change to an $\frac{11}{32}$-inch bit and finish boring the holes through the **verticals**.

16. Bore $\frac{11}{32}$-inch holes all the way through the two remaining **verticals** (A) at the points from step 7; then sand around all the holes to smooth the edges.

17. Repeat steps 1–16 twice to prepare the pieces for the other two panels; be sure to label the pieces from each panel and where they fit so that each joint will match its partner in the final assembly.

18. The hinges that attach the panels of the completed project should sit flush with the faces of the **verticals** (A) to which they're attached. In order to create this fit, you'll need to cut dadoes for the hinges to fit into. Start by determining which of the four **verticals**

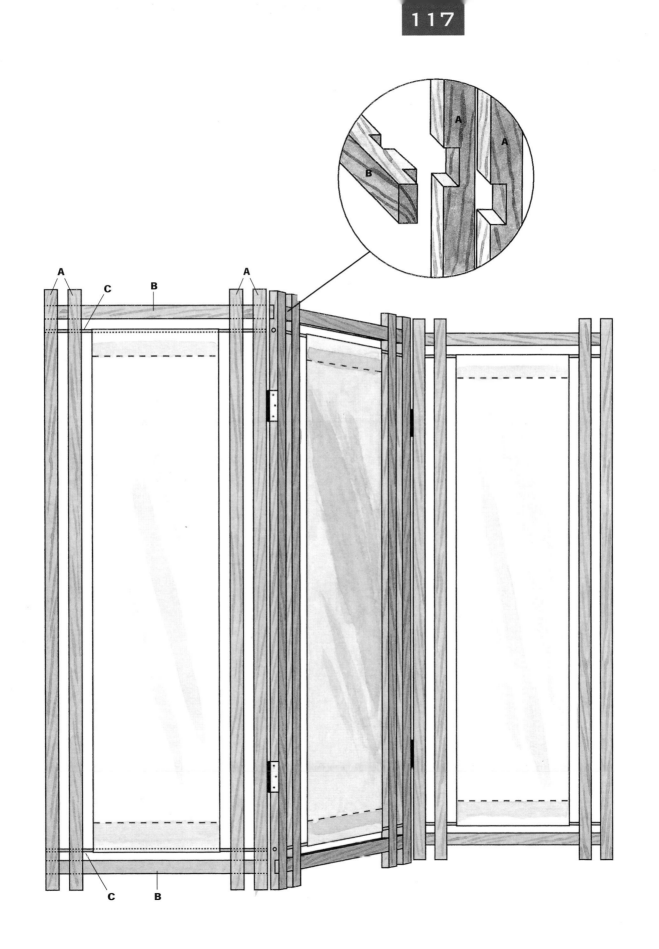

require hinge dadoes; these will be the two outermost **verticals** on the inside panel and the outermost inside **vertical** on each outside panel. (See the illustration for clarification.)

19. Clamp together the four **verticals** (A) that will get hinge dadoes, face-to-face, with the hinge edges up and their ends even.

20. From each end of the four **verticals** (A), measure in 10¼ inches and square a line across all four pieces at this point. From this line, measure over the height of the hinge leaf (using an actual hinge to make this measurement), and square a line across all four pieces at this point.

21. Unclamp the **verticals** (A).

22. Using an actual hinge, mark the depth of each dado to be cut on the edge of the **vertical** (A). This depth will be slightly less than half the thickness of the closed hinge, measured at the barrel.

23. Cut the hinge dadoes, following the same technique described in step 12. If you're using a router, leave the **verticals** (A) clamped, and rout out most of the waste, getting as close as possible to the shoulder lines. Cut back to the lines with a sharp chisel.

24. Reassemble all three panels, but wait until step 30 to install the hinges.

25. Secure the panels by driving a 1¼-inch screw through each half-lap joint. This completes the frame of the sunshade. If you plan to use the project

on grass, drive a tent stake into the bottom end of each **vertical** (A) at this step.

26. Sand the frame smooth; then finish it with a minimum of two coats of a water-based exterior wood finish.

27. Each panel of the sunshade has a rectangular canvas screen, suspended between two **dowels** (C). These screens require some minor sewing. Either do the sewing yourself, or barter woodworking for fabric work with a local sewer. Either way, start by washing and drying the canvas. Then fold the fabric over 1½ inch along each 69-inch edge and press these folds into place. Use a running stitch to close the hem along the edges. Then fold the (now) 14-inch ends over 2½ inches, press these folds into place, and pin them. Wait to sew these hems until you can test the fit on the sunshade.

28. Cut six **dowels** (C).

29. To install the canvas rectangles, start a **dowel** (C) through one set of holes in one set of **verticals** (A) until the dowel comes through on the inside of the panel. Insert the dowel through the proper channel in the canvas rectangle and into the holes on the opposite **verticals** on the panel. Repeat at the other end. The canvas should be stretched tight. If the rectangle doesn't fit properly, adjust the folds at the short ends of the fabric; then sew the hems with a running stitch.

30. Install the hinges. The hinges on the project shown in the photo were installed so that they operate opposite each other; in other words, the knuckles of the hinges show on opposite sides of the sunshade, and they open in opposite directions. This allows the project to fold flat; if you'd prefer that the sunshade be able to open into a U-shape, simply install all the hinges on the same sides

STURDY GARDEN BENCH

Maybe the reason you don't stop and smell the roses more often is that there's nowhere nice to sit while doing so. This attractive bench will solve that problem. Its quiet design will enhance, rather than compete with, your flower garden, and its sturdy construction will offer years of comfortable seating.

DESIGNER: **RALPH SCHMITT**

▼RECOMMENDED MATERIAL

Pressure-treated pine or spruce

▼RECOMMENDED FINISH

Exterior stain

▼MATERIALS

21 linear feet of 4 x 6 PT stock

▼HARDWARE

24 6" timber spikes

▼CUTTING LIST

CODE	DESCRIPTION	QTY.	MATERIAL	DIMENSIONS
A	Feet	2	4 x 6 stock	14½" long
B	Inside bench supports	2	4 x 6 stock	9" long
C	Outside bench supports	4	4 x 6stock	11" long
D	Outer seat pieces	2	4 x 6 stock	46" long
E	Inner seat piece	1	4 x 6 stock	48" long

NOTE: *Due to the thickness of the 4 x 6 timbers, to make cuts you'll need to cut halfway through one face of each timber with a circular saw; then turn the piece over and finish the cut through the other face.*

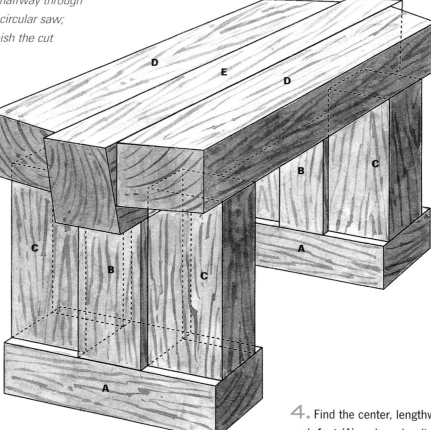

INSTRUCTIONS

1. Cut two **feet** (A).

2. On one face of each **foot** (A), find the center along the timber's width. Mark a line along the length of the piece at this point.

3. From each end of each **foot** (A), measure in and mark points at 1 inch and 4½ inches across the center line. Use a ¼-inch drill bit to bore pilot holes through the **feet** at these points. You'll bore four holes in each **foot** in this step.

4. Find the center, lengthwise, of each **foot** (A) and mark a line across the width of the timber at this point.

5. On both **feet** (A), measure in 1 inch from each edge and mark this point on the line you made in step 4. Use the ¼-inch drill bit to bore pilot holes through the **feet** at these points. You'll bore two holes in each **foot** in this step.

6. Cut two **inside bench supports** (B).

7. Stand an **inside bench support** (B) on end and place a **foot** (A), facedown and edges flush, over it. The end of the **inside bench support** should be centered under the pilot holes from step 5. (See the illustration.) Measure to make sure that the **inside bench support** is exactly in the middle (lengthwise) of the **foot**. Attach the pieces with 6-inch timber spikes through the pilot holes from step 5. Repeat with the remaining **inside bench support** and **foot**.

8. Cut four **outside bench supports** (C).

9. Place two **outside bench supports** (C) under each **foot** (A), one on either side of the **inside bench support** (B), centered widthwise under the **foot**. The inside edge of each **outside bench support** should be against the face of an **inside bench support**, and the outside edge of each **outside bench support** should be flush with the end of the **foot**. (See the illustration.)

10. Attach the **outside bench supports** (C) to the **feet** (A) with 6-inch timber spikes through the pilot holes from step 3.

11. Cut two **outer seat pieces** (D) and one **inner seat piece** (E).

12. To cut the angled ends of the **seat pieces** (D and E), on one edge of each **seat piece** measure and mark $1\frac{1}{2}$ inches from each end. Draw a line from each mark, angling the line across the timber to the other corner at that end. Cut to these lines to make a trapezoid.

13. On each end of the **outer seat pieces** (D), measure in 6 inches from the point and square a line across the face. On those lines and 1 inch in from each edge, bore a $\frac{1}{4}$-inch hole through the **outer seat pieces**, for a total of four holes per piece.

14. On both faces of the **inner seat piece** (E), measure in $5\frac{1}{4}$ inches from the point and square a line across the face there.

15. Stand the bench support assemblies that you completed in step 10 on their **feet** (A), with the **feet** about $38\frac{1}{2}$ inches apart. Place the **inner seat piece** (E), long edge up, on top of the **inside bench supports** (B), with the lines from step 14 at the outside faces of the **outside bench supports** (C).

16. To prevent movement, clamp across the **bench supports** (B and C) right under the **inner seat piece** (E). At a steep downward angle, starting $\frac{1}{2}$ inch above the top of an **outside bench support** (C), bore a $\frac{1}{4}$-inch pilot hole into one face of the **inner seat piece** and toward the center top of one **inside bench support** (B). Bore another $\frac{1}{4}$-inch pilot hole through the same face into the other **inside bench support**.

17. Drive a 6-inch timber spike into each of the angled holes. Remove the clamps.

18. Place the **outer seat pieces** (D) on top of the **outside bench supports** (C), with their long edges against the **inner seat piece** (E), which will protrude about 1 inch at each end.

19. Drive 6-inch timber spikes through all eight of the holes you bored in step 13.

20. Finish the bench as desired, and let it dry; then have a seat and take a rest!

ACKNOWLEDGEMENTS

Creating a book is never a one-person endeavor. I would like to extend my sincere and warm thanks to the following people who helped bring this one together:

All the folks at STERLING PUBLISHING COMPANY (New York), but especially Charlie Nurnburg and Emma Gonzales

The very talented CONTRIBUTING DESIGNERS who are listed separately on page 125

JOE ARCHIBALD (Asheville, North Carolina), for editing the first-round drafts of the more complex projects in this book; for acting as my always-on-call, unofficial technical advisor; for keeping me company during countless late-night and weekend sushi dinners at the office; but most of all, for being such a darn good friend

EVAN BRACKEN (Light Reflections, Hendersonville, North Carolina), whose expertise with a camera brought every project in the book to glorious light, and whose patience and sense of humor made every photo shoot a lark. Unless otherwise credited, all the photos in this book are by Evan.

GENEVIEVE AND LARRY BURDA and the entire staff at Mars Hill Hardware (Mars Hill, North Carolina), for fielding my constant questions about lumber and hardware

AMY COOK (Assistant Editor, Lark Books, Asheville, North Carolina), for her enthusiastic support, impeccable writing, and resourceful research skills

JACKIE FLENNER (Asheville, North Carolina), for producing a comprehensive, reader-friendly index

THOM GAINES (Art Director, Lark Books, Asheville, North Carolina), for giving this book its good-looking, easy-to-use design

GEORGIA PACIFIC CORPORATION, for allowing us to use their gorgeous photos of deciduous and coniferous forests that appear on page 9

ORRIN LUNDGREEN (Asheville, North Carolina), for creating the beautiful illustrations in this book—under tight deadlines, and always with a smile

JAN MENON (Editorial intern, Lark Books, Asheville, North Carolina), for walking through the door every day of her internship with a big smile and a willingness to take on any task

CHRIS RICH (Director of Custom Publishing, Lark Books, Asheville, North Carolina), for her guidance, experience, and unconditional friendship

THOMAS STENDER (Thomas Stender Design, Buffalo, New York), for endlessly checking every project, every illustration, and each step in every set of Instructions to ensure accuracy. I simply could not have produced *Weekend Woodworking for the Garden* without Tom's help!

DIANA STOLL (Asheville, North Carolina), for tackling the difficult job of proofreading a woodworking manuscript

MARK STROM (Lothlorien Woodworking, Asheville, North Carolina), for going far above and beyond what's normally asked and expected of a designer

SKIP WADE (Asheville, North Carolina), for making every project look its best for the camera

For allowing us to tromp through gardens and grounds in pursuit of perfect photographs, thanks to the following ASHEVILLE, NORTH CAROLINA RESIDENTS AND BUSINESSES:

Randy Barrows, Beaufort House Victorian Bed and Breakfast, Diane Claybrook, Hedy Fischer and Randy Shull, Dr. Stewart and Debby Harley, Beth and Karl Lail, Lothlorien Woodworking, Bonnie Sheldon, Collen Sikes, Kay Stafford, Mark and Jo Strom, University of North Carolina at Asheville Botanical Gardens, Dr. Peter and Cathy Wallenborn, Craig Weis, and Ditta Wiener.

Finally, for allowing us to tap their knowledge and their stockrooms, thank you to the following BUSINESSES:

B.B. Barnes (Asheville, North Carolina); Home Depot (Asheville North Carolina); Mars Hill Hardware (Mars Hill, North Carolina); and Lowes (Asheville, North Carolina).

METRIC CONVERSIONS

INCHES	CM	INCHES	CM	INCHES	CM	INCHES	CM
1/8	0.3	5	12.7	22	55.9	39	99.1
1/4	0.6	6	15.2	23	58.4	40	101.6
3/8	1.0	7	17.8	24	61.0	41	104.1
1/2	1.3	8	20.3	25	63.5	42	106.7
5/8	1.6	9	22.9	26	66.0	43	109.2
3/4	1.9	10	25.4	27	68.6	44	111.8
7/8	2.2	11	27.9	28	71.1	45	114.3
1	2.5	12	30.5	29	73.7	46	116.8
1 1/4	3.2	13	33.0	30	76.2	47	119.4
1 1/2	3.8	14	35.6	31	78.7	48	121.9
1 3/4	4.4	15	38.1	32	81.3	49	124.5
2	5.1	16	40.6	33	83.8	50	127.0
2 1/2	6.4	17	43.2	34	86.4		
3	7.6	18	45.7	35	88.9		
3 1/2	8.9	19	48.3	36	91.4		
4	10.2	20	50.8	37	94.0		
4 1/2	11.4	21	53.3	38	96.5		

Volumes

1 fluid ounce = 29.6 ml
1 pint = 473 ml
1 quart = 946 ml
1 gallon (128 fl. oz.) = 3.785 l
liters x .2642 = gallons
liters x 2.11 = pints
liters x 33.8 = fluid ounces
gallons x 3.785 = liters
gallons x .1337 = cubic feet
cubic feet x 7.481 = gallons
cubic feet x 28.32 = liters

Weights

0.035 ounces = 1 gram
1 ounce = 28.35 grams
1 pound = 453.6 grams
grams x .0353 = ounces
grams x .0022 = pounds
ounces x 28.35 = grams
pounds x 453.6 = grams
tons (short) x 907.2 = kilograms
tons (metric) x 2205 = pounds
kilograms x .0011 = tons (short)
pounds x .00045 = tons (metric)

CONTRIBUTING DESIGNERS

Thanks to the talented woodworkers who designed and built projects for this book. When we asked them to come up with simple, yet attractive projects that a beginning woodworker could make, the following folks came through admirably:

JOE ARCHIBALD spends the better part of each day designing homes in Asheville, North Carolina. In his off hours, he goes bike riding in the mountains, entertains his dog Calamity Jane, and runs ArcDesign, a custom woodworking business. Joe built the seedling trays on page 87 and the stunning portable sunshade on page 114.

ROBIN CLARK owns and operates Robin's Wood, Limited, a woodworking studio in Asheville, North Carolina. He's especially well known for his innovative abodes for various beasts. Robin contributed the following projects for this book: the garden tote (page 75); the squirrel feeder (page 50); the butterfly box (page 36); the bluebird house (page 43); the duckboard square (page 68); the duckboard table (page 105); the duckboard bench (page 102); and the potting bench (page 70).

JIM HOWE and his wife, Jan, own and operate Roaring Fork Woodworking Company in Hot Springs, North Carolina. Best known for his cabinetry work, Jim has a gift for transferring his sense of esthetics to functional items; the compost bin on page 81 is an excellent example.

GARY ISRINGHAUS performs custom design work out of his home in Asheville, North Carolina. In addition to his gifts as a designer, Gary is also a talented writer; we look forward to seeing a screenplay with his name in the near future! In the meantime, enjoy his latest creative endeavor, the hanging wine chiller on page 96.

DAVID PENLAND is a co-owner of the Reems Creek Valley Nursery in Weaverville, NC. A noted garden expert, David has an eye for finding materials that others might overlook. David built the gorgeous boot bench on page 90 out of wood he salvaged from an abandoned barn near his home.

RALPH SCHMITT earns his keep designing and building custom wooden furniture and interiors. This is only one of the many books in which his work has been featured. You'll find Ralph's unique take on a picnic table and bench combination on page 108, and his exceptionally sturdy garden bench on page 119.

MARK STROM is a well-known woodworker, sculptor, and artist in Asheville, North Carolina. When he's not gardening at home with his wife, Jo, Mark works at Lothlorien Studio, producing everything from functional garden furniture to fabulous religious statuary. Mark created the following projects for inclusion in this book: the bat abode (page 64); the Oriental plant pedestal (page 39); the elegant planter (page 96); the trellis (page 52); the arbor and bench combination (page 56); and the candleholders (page 100).

BARRY TRIBBLE, who owns Just Wood Custom Millwork, Inc. in Marion, North Carolina, usually works with fine veneers to create custom office interiors. He agreed to take a stab at an outdoor design, and came up with the ingenious wall-mounted tool holder on page 78.

INDEX OF SUBJECTS

INDEX OF PROJECTS